How to Develop
ldren's Early Literacy

How to Develop Children's Early Literacy

A Guide for Professional Carers and Educators

Laurie Makin and Marian Whitehead

P·CP

Paul Chapman Publishing

First published 2004

Paul Chapman Publishing
A SAGE Publications Company
6 Bonhill Street
London EC2A 4PU

SAGE Publications Inc
2455 Teller Road
Thousand Oaks, California 91320

SAGE Publications India Pvt Ltd
B-42 Panscheel Enclave
Post Box 4109
New Delhi 100 017

Library of Congress Control Number: 2003104616

A catalogue record for this book is available from the British Library

ISBN 0 7619 4332 3
ISBN 0 7619 4333 1 (pbk)

Typeset by GCS, Leighton Buzzard, Beds.
Printed in Great Britain by Athenaeum Press, Gateshead

Contents

1 Introduction   **1**
  Greetings to our readers   1
  Meet the authors   1
  How this book is organised   2
  Individual differences in literacy   3
  Early literacy   5
  A quiz to try   7
  Approaches to early literacy   9
  The role of adults in children's early literacy   11
  A literacy snapshot   13

2 Literacy for babies   **15**
  Brainy babies   16
  Real communicators   17
  Sharing books with babies   21
  A case study   25
  Deep literacy roots   27
  A first year with books   27
  Further information   28

3 Literacy for toddlers   **29**
  Children's development between 18 months and 3 years   29
  Supporting toddlers' early literacy   30
  Language development   32
  Positive associations with literacy   39
  Eye-hand coordination and small muscle control   40

Awareness of the many ways literacy operates in homes
and communities   42
A literacy snapshot   43

4 Literacy for pre-school and nursery children   **45**
Some developments in the 3 to 4 years stage   45
Do children learn anything in pre-schools and nurseries,
apart from sharing and getting on with other people?   47
Shouldn't they be sitting down and learning their letters
and sounds?   51
When will they be ready for proper reading books?   56
Using story props   58
A literacy snapshot   59
More about schemas   61

5 Literacy for children in transition to school   **64**
Introduction   64
Literacy-enriched play   67
Observing and building upon individual differences in
literacy learning   69
A literacy snapshot   79

6 Let's think about ...   **81**
Play and literacy   81
Bilingualism and literacy   85
Special needs and literacy   91
Assessment of children's literacy   95
Official curriculum frameworks   100

7 Some useful resources   **107**
Further reading   108
Children's books referred to in the text   109
Professional journals   109
Videos   110
Resource pack   111
Useful addresses   111
A starter collection of picture books   112
Communicating with families about early literacy   113

References   **119**

Index   **121**

Introduction

Greetings to our readers

- Do you look after a child or a group of children between birth and school entry?
- You may be studying for a vocational qualification in early childhood.
- Are you a nursery nurse, teaching assistant or a qualified teacher working with under-5s for the first time?
- Maybe you help out in a nursery or day care centre or preschool.
- You may be just thinking about being or doing one of these things.

If so, this book is for you.

Meet the authors

Laurie Makin is Director of the Children and Education Research Centre at the University of Newcastle in Australia. Laurie has published widely in the area of early literacy, and, in collaboration with colleagues, has produced a number of literacy-related resources for early childhood staff and students. She has two young grandchildren (one 5 years old, one 3 months old, at the time this book was written), so has been able to undertake a refresher course in developing young children's literacy!

Marian Whitehead was formerly Senior Lecturer in Education at Goldsmiths College, University of London. She is the author of several standard texts on the development of language and literacy in the early years. Marian advises schools, care settings, training providers and various publications on ways of working with families and communities to support young children's language and literacy learning. She has four grandchildren, the youngest is 3 and the oldest is 16. All of them have taught her about literacy and featured in her books and articles.

How this book is organised

There are seven chapters in this book. This introduction is the first. Chapters 2 to 5 review the literacy learning of children from birth to school entry. We take a chronological approach to children's early literacy, starting with babies, then toddlers, pre-schoolers and, finally, children in transition to school. In each of these chapters, we look at ideas that will support children's literacy learning and their positive dispositions towards literacy. We include ideas about setting up the environment, providing literacy resources and experiences, and interacting to promote literacy. In Chapter 6 we think about some of the issues in early literacy that need to be considered, whatever the age of the child. The issues we have chosen are:

- play and literacy;
- bilingualism and literacy;
- special needs and literacy;
- assessment of children's literacy in the years prior to school entry and in transition to school;
- official curriculum frameworks outlining expectations relating to literacy.

The final chapter contains information on some additional resources that may be useful. We also include a list of references and an index to help you find information easily.

Throughout the book, we have tried to alternate gender pronouns ('he', 'she', and so on) when it seems necessary to refer to individual children.

Individual differences in literacy

Children are very different in their interests and levels of knowledge about literacy. They will have had many different literacy experiences in their homes and communities before they come to the early childhood setting. One 3-year-old may be reading already. One may be able to use a computer mouse and type her name. One may be totally uninterested in books. Another may love drawing and scribbling and painting. Good educators and carers recognise and respond positively to children's differences. Here are some examples that show the wide range of differences in children's interests and experiences.

Example 1: Two-year-old Dylan developed a passion for sharks after finding pictures of dozens of them on the inside covers (endpapers) of a storybook about a little boy who loved dinosaurs – until he saw a picture of a shark! All Dylan's family and friends had to draw sharks for him and talk about them. He was taken to several big aquariums to see real sharks and friends and family collected leaflets and books about the many different kinds of sharks, which he could soon recognise and name. He also collected lots more storybooks about sharks, some bought for him and some borrowed from libraries. His bath-time toys soon included lots of plastic shark models and many a fearsome underwater struggle took place during his evening bath. Dylan at 2 years of age was helped by his family to become an 'expert' on sharks, in the way that many very young children become experts on trucks, dinosaurs, trains or chickens.

Example 2: Clair, between the ages of 4 and 5, became very interested in computers. Her parents both worked from home and used the computer frequently, so, like most children, Clair wanted to copy her parents. They encouraged a short time on the computer on most days, during which time they would show her something new and then let her explore freely, using her own CD-ROMS. By the time she was 5, Clair was quite knowledgeable about many aspects of computer use.

One day, she was pretending to be a magician and showing her uncle some magic tricks. When he complimented her on her ability, she replied, 'If you want to know more, visit my website at www.magic.com.au.' Clair didn't have her own website, but she

3

1.1 Clair using the computer

knew what they were, how they were used and the format in which they were presented.

Example 3: When she entered preschool, Satoko was a fluent speaker of Japanese and very interested in origami. She enjoyed making simple human and animal origami figures and making up stories about their adventures. When she started preschool, all of the other children spoke English and she was lost and unhappy for the first week or two. Satoko's teacher talked with her parents, with the help of an interpreter, to find out what Satoko liked and was interested in. Knowing this, the teacher was able to introduce origami to all of the children and Satoko's skill became a way in, helping her develop friendships with children who didn't share her language or cultural background.

Example 4: Ben was born with a severe hearing disability. Luckily, this was diagnosed early, and his parents, who were not hearing-impaired, learned sign language as a way of communicating with Ben. When Ben was 3 years old, his mother had to return to work to supplement the family's income. Ben's parents worried a great deal about how he would get on in the long day at the care centre.

With the help of local agencies, they were able to find a centre that had the assistance of a visiting teacher for the hearing-impaired. The educators at the centre decided that they wanted to help all of the children become aware of, and appreciate, different ways of communicating. One of the strategies they used was to make a class book of signs, which interested all the children and led to a wider exploration of non-verbal communication, including facial expression and body language.

All of these children are different from each other in their abilities, their interests and their experiences. The important thing for each of them, whatever their age, cultural background, language, or home and community experiences, is to be with early childhood educators who will find a match, or make links, between that child's knowledge, skills, interests, abilities, and experiences, and the literacy learning environment of the educational setting.

We hope that this book will help you find such matches and links to facilitate children's early literacy and learning, and that you will not hold too rigidly to an age–stage approach to learning.

Early literacy

Have you ever marvelled at how babies can make their wishes very clear, even without words?

> *In picture 1.2 Lilli (3 months) is screaming loudly. When her mother calls out, 'It's OK, Lilli, I'm coming', her cry changes, even though she doesn't understand what her mother is saying.*

Have you heard young children's creative use of language?

> *Clair (3 years 6 months) claims proudly, 'Me gotted it!'*

Have you seen the excitement when a child recognises the first letter of their name?

> *Whenever Morgan (2 years 5 months) sees the MacDonald's sign, she shouts gleefully, 'Look, Mum, that's my letter. We got to get a burger.'*
>
> (Makin and Whiteman, 2002)

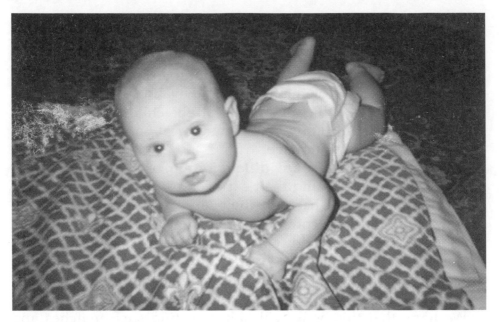

1.2 Lilli hears mum's voice

Has a child ever shown you proudly a page on which they have scribbled, and said,

>   *'Look what I writed'*?

Have you seen a child show you they understand that there is a relationship between pictures on a page and real-life objects?

>   *When his father is reading to Kyle, they come to a picture of a ball. Kyle (14 months) jumps off his father's lap, goes and finds his own ball and brings it back to Dad.*

Have you been surprised and perhaps embarrassed to find that a young child knows more about technology than you do?

>   *Manny (3 years) picks out his favourite video and puts it in the machine. His older brother (8 years) is the only one in the family who can programme the video!*

If you are interested in these things and want to know how to support young children in their literacy learning, this book is for you!

A quiz to try

Try this short quiz. Answer yes or no to each of the statements:

What I think about literacy

1   Literacy is reading and writing.
2   Literacy isn't like it used to be.
3   Literacy starts when children go to school.
4   Literacy starts when children are born.
5   Children's scribbles are important.
6   Children's life opportunities will be related to their literacy.

Let's look at each of these in turn

1   *Literacy means reading and writing.* The answer here is both yes and no. Yes, literacy is reading and writing, but it is now considered to be more than this. Literacy now includes non-verbal communication – gestures and sounds and body language. It includes listening and talking as well as reading and writing. It also includes areas like visual literacy, techno-literacy and critical literacy, all of which we will look at later in this book.

2   *Literacy isn't like it used to be.* The answer here is yes. Just a few years ago, hardly anyone had a home computer, a laptop or a mobile phone or palm pilot. Email wasn't used. The world wide web was just beginning to impinge on people's consciousness. Even more recently, use of literacy tools is changing. For example, young people use SMS (short messaging systems) on their mobile phones more than older people, who tend to use their mobile phone simply as an additional phone.

3   *Literacy starts when children go to school.* The answer here is no, it starts long before this. The literacy experiences children have before they go to school and what they know about literacy are very important. A well-known Australian children's writer called Mem Fox (2001) says, 'The first day of school is almost too late to learn to read. It's as scary as that!' This book will show you how to make sure that children take

7

part in literacy events and practices in ways that are fun and enjoyable, and that are also building strong literacy foundations.

4   *Literacy starts when children are born.* The answer here is yes. If you accept that literacy includes listening and talking, then it starts at birth, if not before. There are reports that babies in the womb who hear the same book over and over – perhaps the favourite of an older sibling – respond positively to that book after birth! It only takes a few days before new babies respond to the voice and smell of the main person who feeds them, cuddles them, changes them and plays with them. Reading to them, while they are cuddled in an adult's lap, can start at any age. Many people think that about 3 months, when they can hold their heads up, is a good time.

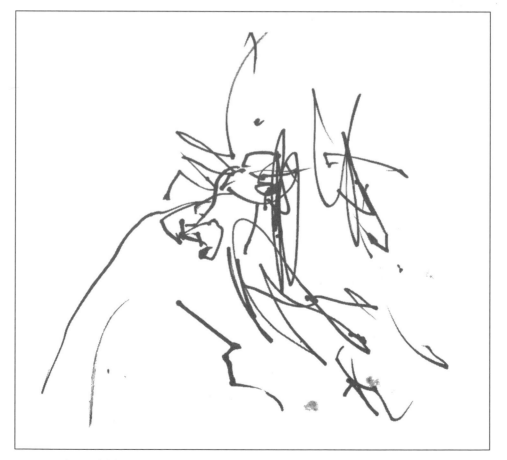

1.3 Early scribble

5   *Children's scribbles are important.* The answer here is yes. They are the child's first attempts at using writing tools to make marks. When the people who are important to them respond positively to what they do, children want to do more. They learn that writing is a valued part of their world. We will look later at how scribble such as that shown in Picture 1.3 develops into 'proper' writing.

6   *Children's life opportunities will be related to their literacy.* The answer here is yes. Problems with literacy are associated with other problems like unemployment and delinquency. Of course, literacy is not a magic bullet and some people who are not literate are very successful. However, on the whole, it makes sense to give children the best start we can.

Approaches to early literacy

Theorists have different ideas about what literacy is, and about when and how it should be taught and learned. Current theoretical perspectives on literacy tend to reflect either a developmental framework coming out of psychology and psycholinguistics (see, for example, Sulzby, 1985/1994) or a sociocultural framework coming out of sociology and sociolinguistics (see, for example, Hill et al, 1998, Makin and Jones Diaz, 2002). There are two approaches to early literacy that underpin the content of this book. One is based on the concept of emergent literacy. The other is based on the concept of literacy as social practice.

Both of these approaches are different from earlier ideas about literacy, which were often based on a concept of reading 'readiness'. A readiness approach reflects a traditional view of literacy as book-based reading and writing, rather then the wider view put forward earlier in this introduction. The role played by children's home and community experiences is largely overlooked in this approach and the emphasis is upon skills development.

If we believe that children's literacy learning begins at birth, and includes talking and listening, a readiness approach is rather narrow, so we will focus on approaches that reflect this wider view and that emphasise the importance of children's home and community experiences as well as their experiences in early childhood settings. We believe that a combination of the approaches to literacy that we have selected has positive potential to provide supportive literacy learning conditions.

Emergent literacy

'Emergent' literacy refers to the literacy knowledge and abilities that children demonstrate before they become conventional readers and writers. In this approach, children are seen as competent and capable from birth. Their early language, their scribbles, their exploration of books, their interest in environmental print, their interactions with technology, are all seen as important demonstrations of their literacy learning.

When we look at literacy from an emergent perspective, we are taking a developmental approach. The limitation of this approach is that the emphasis is on individual children's development. While this is obviously important, we also need to look at why it is that certain groups of children are at particular risk of low literacy. Early childhood settings may support some groups better than others. They may need to change their practices in certain ways to make sure that all children find matches between their home and community experiences and their experiences in early childhood settings.

Literacy as social practice

Think about the young children you know. Where do they see print?

Western societies are full of print – on clothes, cereal packages, posters seen through the window of the car, bus or train, in shops, graffiti, junk mail, TV ads, birthday cards, on signs, on trucks and cars, in shops, even in the sky, as well as in magazines, comics, books, newspapers, computer games, telephone books and so on.

Literacy is how we get things done. It is a very important part of our social practices. Children are active, involved learners from birth. When we look at literacy from the perspective of literacy as social practice, we are taking a social constructivist approach. This means that children build, or construct, knowledge through the social interactions they have within their homes, communities and early childhood settings.

We have said that literacy starts at birth. It is rooted in the ability to communicate. The first places children begin to learn literacy are their homes and communities. A child's first literacy teachers are his family and carers. Children need literacy interactions and experiences from their first days of life.

1.4 Road signs are an example of literacy as social practice

The role of adults in children's early literacy

Literacy starts when adults:

- coo to a baby, sing, say nursery rhymes, play peek-a-boo;
- talk to a baby as if he understands;

- talk about what is happening, what's nearby, feelings as well as actions;
- respond to a baby's attempts (often non-verbal) to communicate with her carers;
- engage a baby in action rhymes;
- read aloud or tell stories.

As children grow older, adults draw their attention to everyday uses of literacy, involve them in everyday experiences such as writing birthday cards, searching the internet, visiting the library, reading books, looking at toy catalogues and so on. Literacy for very young children is not formal teaching, with flash cards or worksheets, or rote learning of the alphabet, or correcting every mistake. It is not hot-housing.

Most experts agree that young children's early literacy is best supported when they:

- have opportunities to learn about the many ways in which literacy is a part of their society;

1.5 Clair and her Dad sharing the newspaper

- are read to frequently;
- have many opportunities to develop their oral language;
- know and enjoy songs and rhymes;
- learn to recognise environmental print such as logos and shop signs;
- develop knowledge of the mechanics of print, for example, that you read from left to right and top to bottom in English;
- have opportunities to play with letters and the sounds they make;
- visit the library often.

In this book, we will look at many ways in which early childhood educators can support early literacy in ways that are appropriate for young children.

A literacy snapshot

This book will take you through from when a baby is born until he starts school. You may like to fill this record out every year for a child who is special to you or for each child in a group of children for whom you care. You may wish to complete it for just one year or for several years.

For the youngest children, you will be deciding on all the information that is recorded. By the time children are 3 or 4, you can discuss it with them and write down what they want you to say. Once they can write their own name and some numbers, they can fill in some of the information themselves.

The literacy snapshot can be completed at any time, but if it is done every year around each child's birthday, you can gradually build up a record to share with the child – immediately and in reflection when she is older, as well as with other people close to the child, such as parents or grandparents, or new carers or teachers.

A literacy snapshot

This is a picture of me.

My name is_____

I am _____ years old

My favourite book is_____

My favourite song is_____

My favourite word is_____

My favourite TV programme is _____

My favourite video/DVD is _____

This year, I have learned how to:

_____

_____

_____

2

Literacy for babies

It may be hard for some readers to believe that we have written a serious chapter about literacy for babies, but we have! We hope to convince you that babies can be involved in sharing some enjoyable activities that are, in fact, the real roots of literacy. But that's as far as the 'seriousness' goes, because we are *not* suggesting that early years practitioners, or families, try to teach babies to read and write. However, you may still be puzzled by this chapter's title. Perhaps you associate literacy with 'sounding out' letters, looking at primers (reading scheme books) and tracing over writing. These methods are probably familiar to you. They are sometimes known as 'formal literacy instruction' and are often used in schools and some early years settings, as you may have seen or remember from your own school days. They are *not* suitable activities for babies and preschool children and we would go further and argue that they are of very limited use in the early years of schooling. What we do in the final part of this chapter, however, is give practical advice on how to start sharing picture books with babies from birth to 18 months. Our main focus is on babies in care and education settings, but the approach we describe is just as suitable for babies when they are in their family homes.

The two themes of the chapter are the amazing abilities of babies and the real roots of literacy, in other words, human communication.

Brainy babies

Recent investigations into how babies think and how their brains develop in the first year of life are at the cutting edge of modern developmental psychology and medicine. In fact, the scientists are just about catching up with the instinctive beliefs of generations of parents, grandparents and childminders around the world that babies:

- understand the people who look after them every day;
- think about what is going on around them;
- enjoy new things and new experiences.

Scientists have known for some decades that babies are born already prepared to find other people interesting and worth communicating with from the start. They are now also able to show that babies' brains are highly adaptable. The main connections in the brains of newborns are not pre-wired or fixed, but are actively linked up as babies respond to being cuddled, fed, changed and talked to by regular carers. This very ordinary stimulation from a few caring people is crucial to brain development, but babies are also stimulated by suitable toys, movements, sounds, shapes and strong colours. Brainy babies develop as caring adults talk to them, cuddle them and have lots of fun with them.

This upsurge of interest in the amazing abilities of babies and toddlers is reflected in a new government-funded project in England, *Birth to Three Matters: A framework to Support Children in their Earliest Years* (DfES, 2002). This is a resource pack consisting of guidance cards and a poster, a video, a booklet and a CD-Rom, intended for practitioners who work with and care for children aged birth to 3. The framework is not an official training package, nor is it a formal curriculum for the under-3s. It is clearly focused on the individual child and on celebrating the young child's potential and competence. It is organised around four aspects of 'the child':

- A Strong Child;
- A Skilful Communicator;
- A Competent Learner;
- A Healthy Child.

These are broad definitions and they look at some very complex aspects of child development. For example, a Strong Child includes the baby's growing awareness of being an individual, the development of self-esteem and a sense of belonging and being cherished. Similarly, a Healthy Child refers to emotional and psychological well-being and the ability to make choices, as well as staying safe and keeping physically fit. Perhaps the complexities of being a Competent Learner and a Skilful Communicator are more obvious and more familiar to early years practitioners. They are certainly central to the approach taken in this book and we will now look more closely at babies as communicators.

Real communicators

The picture of Mattias and his mother demonstrates that pre-verbal babies are skilled at communicating. You can see that at this special moment they only have eyes for each other. You can also see the pleasure on the baby's face, the way he opens his mouth in rhythm with his mother's speech, as if he were about to speak, and you can imagine the special things she is saying to him. It is also

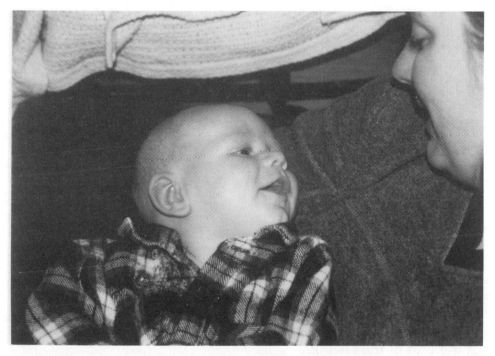

2.1 Mattias, 4 months, and his mother communicating

clear that the baby is an equal partner in the 'conversation' and is encouraging his carer to keep on communicating.

Here is a list of clues that can help us to understand how babies are getting ready for literacy by developing some powerful communication skills.

> *Always listening*
> *The eyes have it*
> *Making faces*
> *Getting excited*
> *Talk to me*

Always listening...

Babies are able to hear before they are born, in fact they have amazingly sensitive hearing in the weeks before birth. Immediately after they are born they show a real preference for the sounds of human voices, picking them out and preferring them to all the other noises in what may seem a noisy and confusing world. Within a very short time babies can identify the voices of their regular carers and turn towards them, or towards the direction from which a familiar voice is coming. Have you noticed that a crying baby can be soothed by a carer's voice, even if it is coming from some distance away? It is clear that baby communicators start with impressively selective hearing skills and begin to take part in little conversations with their regular carers in homes and in care settings.

Babies who are born deaf are also communicators but they will depend on using other senses, such as smell and sight. Several signing systems can be adapted to use with these babies. Parents and professional carers of hearing babies are also finding that a few signs for people, animals, food and everyday activities can be used in conjunction with words in the early months to encourage easy and playful communication. See the 'sing and sign' reference at the end of the chapter.

The eyes have it...

The picture of Mattias and his mother gazing into each other's eyes shows what language and child development experts call 'non-verbal communication'. It reminds us that to get into a conversation with another person usually involves catching their eye to get their attention and frequently looking at them while we communicate. We do know that newborn babies find the eyes the most interesting part of the human face and they gaze into the eyes of their carers when they are wide awake and ready to communicate and play. Interestingly, babies can also let us know that they are tired or bored by switching their focus elsewhere, closing their eyes or turning their faces away.

So baby communicators know how to use eye contact to hold the attention of their carers in a 'conversation' and they know how to switch off.

Babies with impaired vision will start to communicate by reacting to the voices of their regular carers and to the feel of their skin and their familiar smell. Touch and smell are very important ways for *all* babies get to know and recognise their families and a small number of professional carers. However, it is easy to forget that these senses are important starting points for babies' social interactions and the development of other communication skills, like language and literacy, for example.

Babies with impaired hearing will rely on the use of eye contact to get in touch with their carers and should be helped to enjoy lots of close face-to-face talk and play, including appropriate touching, exaggerated facial expressions, natural gestures and a few simple signs taken from international systems such as British or American Sign Language (BSL, ASL) or Makaton.

Making faces...

Adults do tend to go in for exaggerated facial expressions and noises when they talk to babies and play little games with them. We might notice this as we watch other people communicating with babies, or see it on videos and in photos. What is going on here? Well, most parents, carers, professional early years workers and even older children seem to concentrate quite naturally on helping a baby get over the initial problem of not understanding the actual words people are using. So, we are all likely to go in for a bit of over-acting to get across the meanings of our words and intentions – it is a bit like communicating with a person who does not speak our language! We particularly exaggerate the kinds of facial expressions that reflect the feelings and meanings behind our words (raised eyebrows; eyes wide open; mouth gaping; lips pouting; frowning and smiling). We also repeat words much more frequently than is normal in a conversation and pronounce them very slowly. All this dramatic behaviour helps to hold a baby's attention and it makes early communication exciting and full of meaning.

Getting excited...

All the fun and excitement of communicating with a baby makes it easy for adults to want to get involved, and babies usually respond totally to this attention, with their whole bodies. You can actually see the excitement and energy pulsing through them as they wave their arms, open and shut their fingers, stiffen and arch the trunk, kick their legs and wriggle their toes. Perhaps this level of whole body communication and excitement will never again be as noticeable after conventional words develop, but it can still be found in the dancing, the drama and the ceremonies and rituals of human cultures around the world. Later in this chapter we are going to suggest that carers can dance, sing and enjoy many kinds of music with babies.

Another way in which the pleasure and excitement of communication is expressed by babies is with the sounds they can make with their mouths. This can be anything from squeals, grunts, blowing bubbles, hiccups and giggles, to babbling, gurgling and crying for attention and company. You may have been told that these are just accidental noises, indigestion or 'wind', but they can become real communication if you respond to them enthusiastically and treat them as a baby's way of getting into a conversation with you.

Talk to me...

Yes, it's as simple as that! If you can treat the babies you care for as interested and interesting communicators you will give them the best possible start to literacy. The one thing that makes a difference to children's language and literacy development and later success at school is the amount of ordinary daily talk directed especially to them. And we really do mean the ordinary talk about what's going on, where you're going, what you are doing, and comments on what you see as you walk out, visit the store or supermarket, enjoy bath-times, use the computer, prepare food, wash clothes and clean the nursery or home. It is particularly important that the staffing levels and routines in care settings make it possible for key practitioners to direct their talk to individual babies and toddlers and share interactions with them. Basic daily routines like nappy changing can be transformed if we take the opportunity to talk to the baby, offer a small toy or bunch of keys to hold, explain what we are doing and make the baby feel special and valued. Bathing babies after a session of body painting can offer the same chance to turn a care routine into a stimulating social, emotional, linguistic and cognitive experience!

On those occasions when the television is on you still need to watch with babies and toddlers and, afterwards, talk about what you have all seen. Try to join in with any songs and rhymes and link the TV activities to things you and the children know about in your world and organise some similar follow-up activities.

Sharing books with babies

You may be tempted to ask, 'What is the point of reading to babies? What sense can they possibly make of books?'

In fact, there are many good reasons for reading to babies. Just sharing a picture book with a baby is a great opportunity for getting into more communication, more talk, lots of cuddles and a really close look at pictures. A book is also one of the simplest and best toys we can offer a child, after all, it doesn't need a power supply or lots of storage space.

The best reason for sharing books with babies is that it is very enjoyable and this great pleasure shouldn't ever be spoilt by pressure from anyone to teach babies and toddlers to read.

Of course, books are 'educational' and sharing them from the earliest months of life will give a baby an excellent start to communicating, talking, reading and writing. Books will also help you and the babies in your care learn a lot about the wider world and you will never be stuck for something to talk about!

You can also rest assured that there is plenty of reliable evidence that sharing picture books with babies and toddlers lays the foundations for success with school literacy. If news about this important 'root' of literacy doesn't seem all that surprising, you might be interested in some rather more unusual 'off-shoots'. Babies who have shared books at home with their carers also make a flying start in mathematics and science by the time they are 7 and 8 years old. This information comes from a careful study of parents and babies in the city of Birmingham, England, who were given free books and poetry cards and asked to share them every day at home and join the local public library. This project is called Bookstart and has spread throughout the UK and involves families from all kinds of different ethnic, educational and economic backgrounds.

We believe that books are wonderful for babies but we would not want them to push other toys and experiences out of their daily lives, so care and education settings, as well as homes, should never deny babies the pleasures of soft toys, old bags and boxes, mud, sand, water, leaves, shells, cooking pots and lids, bricks, rattles and blankets!

What do babies get from books?

Cuddles and stories
The babies in your care will soon associate books and storytelling with love, security, closeness and pleasure. They will also hear a special story language that has very satisfying rhythms and repetitions. These good feelings about language, stories and books can last a lifetime.

Pictures
Looking at the pictures in books and talking about them helps babies make sense of what is going on in a book. It is the start of learning to create stories that give meanings to pictures. Looking very closely at pictures also develops the useful literacy habit of concentrating on tiny details. This becomes very important when older children start to become readers and look at words, letters and small changes in groups of letters.

Black marks
The little black marks we call print are of great interest to many

babies as they can see them very distinctly. Babies who are shown lots of books, magazines and other print gradually begin to understand that the 'black marks' are also telling a story.

Remember that enjoying cuddles and stories and pictures and print with professional carers and family members helps babies to get the message that literacy is about communication and pleasure.

How is sharing a book with a baby done?

It is usual to make a start once you judge that a baby has become adjusted to your setting and knows one or two key practitioners (see below). Babies at home can be introduced to some books just as soon as their carers have settled down to life with baby!

Find a calm moment when a baby is awake and ready to communicate and play.

Find a fairly quiet place – try it without the TV on whatever the setting – and avoid any other distractions nearby, like musical instruments or crashing building blocks! This is a special time just for the baby and a familiar carer. If you care for several babies, still try to organise times when you can share books with individual babies.

Keep it very brief, especially at first, and let the baby's interest guide you.

A little singing, bouncing, tickling or dancing around makes the book even more fun.

Be really comfortable indoors and outdoors – you and the baby can lie down, curl up under a blanket or in the shade, or just sit how and where you like. Books are to be enjoyed.

Hold the book close to the baby's focus – just a few inches in the early months – and close enough to be touched or sniffed by the baby. Books are for touching, smelling and even tasting!

Turn the pages slowly and talk about what is going on in the story and the pictures. Watch the baby closely and try to let her set the pace for when to turn over and how much to talk. Change bits of the story in the book so as to make it seem to be about this baby and her world. Ask the baby a few questions and point out some interesting things in the pictures. Don't forget to enjoy making a bit of a fool of yourself by using different voices and animal noises, this all helps to bring the book to life.

You will only need a few books that you use again and again in the early days of book sharing. Babies and toddlers love to get really familiar with their books and will soon demand lots and lots of re-readings of their favourites.

As you are going to do a lot of re-reading, try to choose some books that really appeal to you and make you want to talk about the pictures, or the things that are going on.

Store the collection of books for babies low down in a basket or on a shelf so that once babies start to crawl they can find the books and look at them at any time of the day.

Key practitioners

Babies and young toddlers who come into a group setting for the first time need a very gradual introduction to the non-family adults who care for them. They cannot cope with varied numbers of adults who come and go and they must have one 'special' or key person to relate to in the early weeks and months. This person will remain special for them, even when their social contacts increase, and provide a bridge between home and group setting. The key practitioner can be thought of as the person who keeps all the special intimate knowledge about the child (Goldschmied and Jackson, 1994). This is the person who welcomes and settles the child every day, does many of the essential care routines, and gets to know the child's temperament, her likes and dislikes, little habits, cultural background and home experiences. The key practitioner is *not* a parent substitute but a wonderful additional carer who always looks out for the child in the group setting, liaises with any outside agencies (like welfare or health specialists), and enriches the life of the individual child and her family.

Problems?

I'm not very good at reading

Don't worry, a baby doesn't know this and will still love this special time. Let the books and the pictures do their work and turn you into a creative storyteller who is having a good time.

I can't read English easily

You can use the pictures to help you invent your own stories and many picture books do not have any text (print) at all – or very little. Be confident about talking about books in your home language, or other languages you share with the children, and tell the children the traditional stories of your childhood, your community and your culture. Invite parents and family carers from specific language communities in to the setting to tell stories and sing lullabies and songs with the babies and toddlers.

I have several babies in my early years setting
You can certainly have some enjoyable times with a small group of babies and toddlers who are sharing books together, turning the pages and telling each other what is happening in the stories. But try to make it possible, as we suggested above, for each baby to have a short time alone with a key adult and a book. These special times do make a difference to later literacy success in school and should be given a high priority.

We can't afford to buy many books
Try to borrow books, or video and audio story tapes from libraries. Take small groups of children to library storytelling sessions. Ask about local schemes to give literacy advice to carers and free books to young children (there are lots). Make your own simple group books using photos and drawings stuck in scrapbooks, photo albums or even on sheets of paper stitched or clipped together. Invite the children's families in to make simple books about their own babies.

A case study

Dylan and his books (Whitehead, 2002)

This is a study of a baby boy living in London with his English mother and American father who shared picture books with his parents and grandparents from the age of 8 weeks. The study follows Dylan's development and adventures with books up to his 3rd birthday, but there are some interesting observations of what went on in the first 18 months. Right from the start Dylan was involved with all kinds of print, not just picture books, because his carers often held him while they looked at newspapers, magazines, TV listings, adult books, etc. From 3 months Dylan was a very noisy and pro-active book sharer! He would gurgle, squeal, kick his legs, bang the pages and scrabble on the paper with his fingers. By 8 months a real sense of humour emerged as Dylan

2.2 Dylan, 9 months, looking at a catalogue on his own

giggled helplessly when the animals in his favourite book fell out of a big bed with 'thuds', 'bumps' and 'crashes'. Dylan would watch the face of anyone reading to him very closely and also scan the illustrations slowly and thoroughly, as if searching for clues about how the story was going.

By 9 months Dylan liked to read quietly on his own and his favourite position was on his back with a book or magazine held up over his head. He now sounded as if he was reading because his vocalisations were varied, rhythmic and very expressive. At the start of his second year Dylan had a few favourite books that he looked at and listened to over and over again. Some of these were so important to him that he took them to bed with him and could not settle unless he knew exactly where they were. He always liked to sit with a little pile of books to look at, especially after meals, naps and bath time. By 16 months he made all the appropriate noises for the animals in his books and started to name the objects in book illustrations and he particularly enjoyed 'First Word Books' and ABCs. When Dylan was 18 months old the household reflected his passion for 'books with everything' as little collections of books appeared everywhere. In his bedroom there were books in a box alongside two comfy floor cushions; there was a magazine rack of books in his parents' bedroom for early morning visits; a basket of books was next to his toy-box in the living room and more picture books were on the family book shelves. Then, of course, there were little books attached to his buggy and plastic books among the bath toys.

Deep literacy roots

In the first year of a baby's life we can make sure that the roots of literacy go deep by doing some other fun things, as well as sharing books.

- **Play with language** – really enjoy the sounds that babies make and try mucking about with language yourself. Just exaggerate words, names and noises and go in for lots of rhythm and repetition.
- **Sing and dance** – enjoy all kinds of songs, music, clapping, stamping and dancing with the babies in your care. Use these songs, noises and rhythms in the stories you tell or read.
- **Share rhymes and poetry** – sing or recite verses that have good rhymes, nonsense words and tongue-twisters (these rely on words starting with the same sounds), or bits of songs, poems, chants and hymns you remember.

These may seem strange things to do, but they develop young children's love of language and their understanding of how it works.

A first year with books

You might enjoy keeping a record of a baby's first year with books. This can be done for a baby at home or in a care setting. If you are a key practitioner for one baby, or several, in a setting you should share this record with the child's family and with your professional colleagues. Parents who choose to do this at home might like to share it with the child's first professional carers or teachers.

Our first year with books

Some books we liked _____

_____

Favourite pictures in our books _____

_____

What_____BABY'S NAME_____ liked to do with books

_____

Our favourite rhymes, songs, dances, music _____

_____

Baby's first sounds _____

Baby's first words _____

Baby's favourite games, noises, actions _____

_____

What _____BABY'S NAME_____ laughed at _____

_____

Further information

Brainy babies

Gopnik, A., Meltzoff, A. and Kuhl, P. (1999) *How Babies Think.* London: Weidenfeld & Nicolson.

Signing with hearing babies

Video: Felix, S. (2001) *Sing and Sign. Help your Baby to Communicate before Speech.* www.singandsign.com

Literacy for toddlers

Children's development between 18 months and 3 years

The period from 18 months to 3 years is one of rapid development – physically, cognitively and emotionally. By the age of 2 years, children's brains weigh 75 per cent of what they will weigh as adults. This physical growth reflects changes in the structure and functions of the brain, which have important implications for children's early literacy learning.

There has been a great deal of interest in brain development over the past few years. Most people now accept that the first three years of a child's life are critically important. Some people go further. They believe that, in the first three years, there is a window of opportunity for learning that then slams shut. If this is true, it means that, if children don't have certain experiences within the first three years, it will negatively affect them for the rest of their lives. Our view is that this is over-stating the case. Human beings are very resilient. Nevertheless, the first three years of life are certainly very important, in early literacy as in everything else. What happens between the ages of 18 months and 3 years can establish strong literacy foundations for later success in school literacy, and for a love of literacy that is life-long.

Children are very curious about their environment and about what things are called, what they do or are used for, and their characteristics, for example, size, shape, colour, weight, texture.

They are very mobile now. They learn to walk well, run, jump, and climb stairs. They can climb on swings and slides. Some, by the age of three, can pedal a tricycle. This all helps them explore their environment. It can also get them into a lot of trouble! Adults need to provide challenging but safe environments for children to explore.

Supporting toddlers' early literacy

In terms of literacy learning, adults need to offer children opportunities to develop:

- their language, both receptive – that is, what children understand, even if they do not say much – and productive, that is, what children can say;
- positive associations with literacy, and positive dispositions to engage in literacy experiences. There is no point being able to read and write if you have no interest in doing these things. Children should associate literacy experiences with fun, enjoyment and satisfaction;

3.1 Conor imitates the actions of his mother

3.2 Monty, 18 months, looking at a book

- their eye-hand coordination and fine motor control. These become increasingly important later, when children start school. Pencils are smaller than big crayons or paintbrushes, so we usually start off with large markers that are easy for toddlers to grasp. Differences between letters (for example, 'b' and 'd') need close attention to detail. Attention to detail for toddlers often begins with their interest in picture books;

- their awareness of the many ways in which literacy operates in their homes and communities. Different communities use different languages and dialects. Even within the same linguistic community, there may be many different sets of literacy practices. Sometimes these are related to gender and age, as well as to the lives people live, the jobs they have and so on.

In the following sections, we offer some ideas about what you can do in each of the areas listed above to support young children's literacy between the ages of 18 months and 3 years.

Language development

Contexts for talking and reading with toddlers

Talking and reading with toddlers is the best way to help them extend their language. You can talk with children about many things. They are very interested in themselves and their activities! Adults and older children can describe for them in words what they are doing, hearing, seeing, touching, tasting, smelling and feeling.

There seems to be an explosion of vocabulary between about 18 and 22 months. This may be because children become aware that everything has a name. This is the time when the constantly repeated cry of 'What's that?' can drive adults to distraction. However, patience is rewarded as communication increases, along with the child's language. Children's increased memory ability helps them with long words, even if they don't always come out correctly. Ben's version of 'hippopotamus' came out as 'pitohapamus'. He had the right number of syllables and all the right sounds, but not the order. Children have enough grammar now to get most of their meaning across to an adult who knows them well and who listens attentively.

With a focus on naming, the environment needs attention. To name things, we need things to name. So review the environment for textures, colours, and so on, and change what is on display as they become so familiar that pictures, books, displays and so on are not noticed any more.

Children under the age of 3 will not usually start school for another two or three years. However, they are already beginning to learn many aspects of literacy that will help them later. An important predictor of successful school literacy is what is called 'phonological awareness'. This refers to an awareness of sounds and an ability to play with the sounds in a word, separating them out, putting them together, and substituting new sounds to make new words. Later, well-developed phonological awareness will help children decode new words and learn to spell. Children take their first steps towards developing phonological awareness as they are sung to, hear nursery rhymes, engage in action rhymes like 'This little pig went to market', and enjoy alliteration, for example, 'Peter, Peter, pumpkin eater' (Edens, 1998).

Much discussion with toddlers can take place during shared reading experiences. It is now believed that the talk that takes place during shared reading is as important as the reading itself. Book reading is very important. It is also important to include a wide range of books – information books, fairy tales, songbooks, storybooks. However, books are not, and should not be, the only reading experiences children engage in. There are many different text types used in everyday life, for example, toy catalogues, cereal boxes, photo captions, signs, and so on, which all offer opportunities for shared reading, and which help develop children's awareness of the many functions of literacy in society.

Strategies for talking and reading with children

Talk to children about things that they are interested in and are experiencing
The amount of talk directed to a child is related to the child's language development – the more language they hear, the more they learn. However, just any talk doesn't do. If what children hear is mainly commands to do things or not to do things, or negative comments on their actions or personalities, they are not likely to want to join in the talk and extend it! Quality is even more important than quantity. When both are present, the child is in a supportive atmosphere for language learning.

Talk about what is currently being experienced by the child, and about whatever is the focus of joint attention between adult and child. Shared knowledge makes communication much more relevant and easily comprehended on both sides.

Take advantage of everyday opportunities for interaction
Staff can sit with children in small groups at mealtimes and talk with them, rather than simply monitoring the giving out of food.

Children wake from their naps at different times. This can be a lovely time for a quiet chat with individual children. It is very important that children have frequent opportunities for one-to-one interactions with responsive adults.

Time spent looking at the illustrations in different types of print is another rich source of conversation and language growth. Toddlers need unhurried time to take in the details of pictures. Make sure that pictures and print around the room are at the children's eye level, not at an adult's eye level.

Respond positively to what the child says
Also model what you want him to be able to say later. Young children between 18 months and 3 years are beginning to put words together. At first, they may speak 'telegraphically'. This means that they have the main words needed to communicate, but not the fine details. For example, they may say 'Want milk', instead of 'I want a glass of milk, please.' Adults can help children develop their language skills by using two main strategies. One is to expand what the child has said. In response to the previous statement by a child, an adult might say, 'You want a glass of milk, do you?' The other is to both expand and extend what the child has said. In this case, the adult might say, 'You want a glass of milk, do you? I guess you're thirsty. It's a hot day.'

Model what you want the child to say eventually rather then correcting her
It is very common at this stage for children to over-generalise, saying things like 'runned' or 'mouses'. Children are very resistant to direct correction at this time. It seems that somewhere within their brain, rules for generating plurals or past tenses are being worked out. If they hear the correct word in relevant contexts often enough, they will gradually work out what is the correct version.

Check children's receptive understanding
This will help you understand what the child knows and doesn't know at any particular time. Children understand a lot more than they can say. You can do this checking in everyday contexts, for example, you might ask a child to bring you the *blue* cup, or, during shared book reading, you might play games of finding people or objects in the illustrations.

Read to children every day – individually or in small groups of two or three

Children learn many words through listening to stories, but they seem to learn much more if the book-reading is interactive. They need to be able to ask and answer questions, look at the pictures, decide when to turn the page and when to stop the experience. One or two children only is enough. The talk that happens during shared book-reading is as important as the reading itself.

By the end of the second year, many toddlers can follow simple stories, and are beginning to understand that there is a relationship between what happens and how someone feels or what they do. Toddlers enjoy short, simple stories, with pictures that are clearly related to the text. Books that include repeated phrases or rhyming patterns encourage toddlers to anticipate what is coming next and begin to join in. Adults can link what happens in the book with events or feelings known to the child, and can start to ask simple questions that encourage the child to remember the sequence of events in the story.

Develop books of labelled photos showing experiences the child knows

This might include a typical day or an excursion or how to build a tower of blocks. Read them often and talk about them with the child. Photos can also be used for classification and finer distinctions, for example, a book about brushes – hair brushes, shoe brushes, toothbrushes, clothes brushes – being used by the children in the group. Make sure that the child's name is included in the labelling, for example, 'Mandy is brushing her hair with a hair brush.'

Tell stories as well as reading them

Young children enjoy stories about their day, which at this stage do not need plots, simply sequences. Told stories let children see things in their minds the way they want to see them. Instead of reading a bedtime story, an adult can recount the child's day – 'Once upon a time there was a little girl named Mandy. She lived with her mummy and her daddy in a little white house with a kitten called Fluffy. One day, after breakfast, Mummy and Mandy got into the car and drove to day care. Mrs Noble was glad to see Mandy and said, 'Hello, Mandy. We've got something special to do today",' and so on until they get home again. It may sound somewhat unexciting to the rest of us, but it is of absorbing

3.3 Shea plays mum

interest to the child who features as the central character in the story!

Encourage the child to act out real and imaginary scenarios
Although the children are very young, this is the time when imagination begins to inspire children's play (see Picture 3.3). They can have fun acting out some of the roles in familiar stories or television programmes or nursery rhymes. This is a good time to introduce puppets. Dolls and stuffed toys can take on many roles. A big box can be a theatre or television. Pretend play helps children work out how the world around them operates, what different people do and how they behave. Remember that children often confuse reality and fantasy. Mario and his playmates were taking part in a movement activity in which they were invited to pretend that they were clothes being washed in a washing machine. Then they were hung on the line to dry. This involved holding up their arms while the teacher 'pinned' them to an imaginary line. Lunch arrived and the other children ran off. Mario remained where he was and began to cry as he saw the others depart. When the teacher asked him what was the matter, he replied through his tears, 'You didn't unpin me.'

Take neighbourhood walks
This can include different areas of the early childhood setting and the immediate neighbourhood. Point out signs, letterbox numbers and so on. You may also be able to include regular trips to the local library. Photos taken on these walks can be used for sequencing, discussion of signs and purposes (for example, road signs that indicate a crossing, or that people have to stop and wait until cars go by), and for class books.

Think beyond the obvious
Children may learn 'arm', for example, but may not know 'elbow' and 'wrist'. Melissa bumped her elbow and held it up for a kiss, saying, 'Kiss my dis [this part of me].' Remember that faces have chins and cheeks and eyebrows as well as eyes, noses and mouths.

Sing songs
This has many benefits. Children enjoy rhyme, rhythm and repetition. They enjoy joining in chants. Some children may even make up their own chants or songs. Songs and rhymes help

children start to tune in to the sounds in language (phonological awareness). Between the ages of 2 and 3, children are able to join in more complex songs that include different verses, numbers, choruses, and different sounds, for example, 'Old MacDonald'. They learn many words by joining in action rhymes, for example, opposites like high and low or loud and soft. Songs can also be a way of exploring feelings, for example, 'If you're happy and you know it.'

Begin to point out letters and numbers
Use simple ABC and number books. Sing alphabet and number songs. Have magnetic letters and numbers and a magnet board available. Many children by the age of 3 will recognise the first letter in their own name and will joyfully claim 'their' letter when they see it on signs or in printed material.

Make sure that they have many opportunities to see their name in print – on their belongings, their artworks, their scribbles, their storage areas and so on. Draw their attention to their name and the sound it starts with, but do this casually and incidentally, for example, when you're reciting 'Miss Polly had a dolly', you might say, '"Polly" starts with the same sound as your name, Peter.'

Talk about emotions and feelings
Children are often frustrated at this stage at the gap between what they want to do and what they are able to do. 'ME do it!' is a common protest when an adult tries to help. The 'terrible 2s' is a description many adults can relate to. 'No!' and 'Mine!' are the words used most often by many children. The children's emotions are strong and growing more complex, but they have limited coping strategies. One strategy to help them through literacy activities is to make sure that they hear the words that are needed to describe what they feel. Children can begin to talk about their needs and feelings when they have the words they need to do so. Books can help a great deal in this regard – not at the moment of frustration or anger, but later, when things are calmer. Read books that show characters the child can relate to who have felt similar emotions and found a solution. For example, Pat Hutchins' book, *It's MY Birthday!*, shows a little monster (literally!) refusing to share his birthday presents with the other little monsters. He learns that he has much more fun when they all play together.

Positive associations with literacy

It is essential that young children have strong relationships with warm, caring, responsive adults. This is a challenge, especially if children are in multiple care situations, or if there are many part-time or casual staff within an early childhood setting. The experiences that promote literacy at this stage also offer opportunities to build positive, empathetic relationships with children. It is of critical importance for staff in early childhood settings to establish a situation in which children can relate consistently and trustingly to a small number of caring adults. By the age of 2 or 3, children who feel loved and secure seem better able to relate to others, to play imaginatively, to persist enthusiastically in achieving their goals and seem generally more content (Berndt, 1997).

It is good to know that the thought and effort that goes into building warm, secure environments for children also contributes to building strong literacy foundations. Talking with children, cuddling them for a story, or singing to them builds close, trusting relationships as well as promoting positive associations with literacy. It is very important that such experiences are child-focused and experienced by children as individuals or in a small group of only two or three. One person has described trying to get a group of toddlers to sit on a mat to listen to a story as 'like trying to plait sawdust.' Of course, the message is that one shouldn't be trying to plait sawdust! Neither should one be trying to read to children of this age in group situations.

Enjoyment should be paramount when children are engaging in literacy activities. This is not a stage at which to 'teach' them. They will learn a great deal, but they need to have some control of the situation. If adult and child are enjoying an activity, continue it, but if either, and, in particular, the child, starts to show boredom, frustration, tiredness, or lack of interest, it's time to stop.

Build positive partnerships between families and educarers. This helps optimise the support given to children's early literacy. Strategies can include informal chats, special days (for example, a grandparents' day), communication books, surveys, newsletters, an open door policy, evening functions and a small borrowing library.

Eye-hand coordination and small muscle control

Strategies

Provide access to writing materials

At this stage, children are developing their eye-hand coordination and the control of their fine muscles. This means that they can hold a marker and are beginning to make controlled marks. They begin to copy adults when they scribble so that, for example, if the language they hear and see most is English, they will begin to scribble lines that go from left to right and from top to bottom.

Toddlers need access to markers such as crayons, chalk and paint brushes, and to different types of writing surfaces such as paper (unlined, in different colours and textures) and chalkboards; and they need encouragement to use these. Children's early scribbles are the first steps to writing. Respond positively – show interest in their scribbles, share them with others, display them.

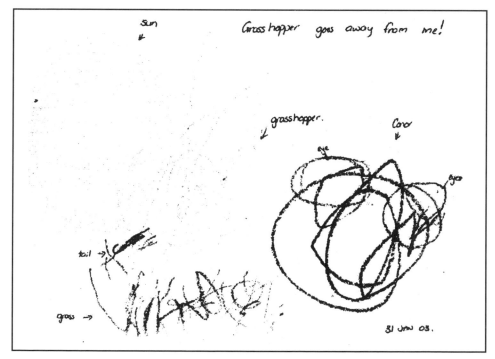

3.4 Grasshopper

Include many fine motor activities

There are many experiences which, although not directly related to literacy, help children develop the fine motor skills and the attention to detail that will stand them in good stead when they begin more formal literacy learning. These include finger painting, brush painting, threading, doing puzzles, playing with stacking and nesting toys, and building with blocks. Dancing with streamers or tossing beanbags are other example of activities that help children develop hand-eye coordination and fine motor control.

Include songs, books, action rhymes and finger plays that involve the child physically

Any book offers opportunities to hold the book, turn the page, or point to things. Some books offer children opportunities to lift flaps or pull tabs, for example the 'Spot' books, or Jan Ormerod's *Peek-a-Boo!*. Others, like Zita Newcome's *Toddlerobics Animal Fun*, involve young children in 'toddler gymnastics' – leaping, jumping, clapping, hopping and so on. Children can start to join in actions in songs like Hokey Pokey, Where is Thumbkin? and London Bridge.

Share book handling with children

From a very early age, children can turn pages very dexterously if they have opportunities to practise this. They can find the beginning of the story and the end, and hold the book themselves while the adult reads.

Use messy play

Most children enjoy playing with Goop or playdough, mud, finger painting and foot painting. A word of caution – around the time that they are mastering toilet training, some children do not want to engage in messy play. They will return to their enjoyment of it at a later stage, so provide different experiences which they are happier with and which also develop the skills being focused upon, for example, rolling out dough, washing doll clothes, painting a wall with water.

Awareness of the many ways literacy operates in homes and communities

One example of the concept of literacy as social practice is clearly seen in the changes in literacy tools during the past 50 years. Many older people today grew up in a world without television. Now the majority of households have a television, and increasing numbers of people have home computers, video recorders, DVD players, mobile phones and so on. What is sometimes called 'techno-literacy' plays an increasingly important role in everyday literacy.

How does this affect very young children? Many young children seem mesmerised by TV, which is often used as a welcome, free babysitter for exhausted adults. Canny marketing aims programmes even at children as young as 18 months (Teletubbies, for example). Other programmes watched by children may be full of advertisements aimed directly at them. Research into the effects of television on young children is mixed. Negative findings relate to increased passivity, less interest in books, decreased imagination, reduced language learning and slower development of an awareness of dimensionality – TV screens are two-dimensional, whatever is shown on them.

Some researchers state that children under the age of 2 years should not be exposed to television at all. This is probably unrealistic in today's world, but it does seem important to have guidelines relating to what is watched and for how long. It is also important for an adult to watch with a child and to talk to the child about what he is seeing. This is particularly important when it comes to violence, whether children see it in cartoons or soap operas or news bulletins.

Children between 2 and 3 years can begin to join in many household activities that develop their language and their awareness of ways in which literacy is used in their homes and communities. Their experiences should be as 'authentic' as possible. Sometimes objects like chairs, tables and walls in early childhood settings are labelled with words written on cards. This is not authentic, in other words, it is not showing children how literacy is used in everyday life and is not helpful. On the other hand, having a sign on a cupboard saying 'Art Materials' is authentic and helpful (for those who can read the sign!).

There are many authentic literacy experiences in which children can participate. For example, in early childhood settings, it is common for parents to sign their children in and out when they bring their child to the centre or nursery. Toddlers enjoy having their own sign-in book, which can be placed beside their parents' book. They will make a mark or draw a picture or do a scribble. They don't need to be able to write 'properly' to take part in such experiences.

Cooking is an activity loved by most young children. They can measure, pour, stir, and observe the changes between raw and cooked foods. They can also be introduced to recipes. They can help write shopping lists, fill out banking forms, follow simple maps (try a simple treasure hunt), make signs, play with a computer mouse and so on.

Go on neighbourhood 'literacy walks'. Have fun searching for numbers on letterboxes, cars and shop signs. Look for logos and familiar shop signs. Take photos to use later in discussions of the neighbourhood, transport, where children live and so on. Sort the photos into places that are close to the day care centre or not so close.

A literacy snapshot

You may want to keep a record of some information about the tremendous literacy learning that takes place between 18 months and 3 years. If you work in an early childhood setting, you may use children's birthdays or certain times of the year such as the end of the year as the time when the snapshot is taken. If you are at home with one or more toddlers, you may make a different record at the end of the second year, and another at the end of the third year. Here is a suggested format.

My literacy snapshot

This is a picture of me in the year _____

My name is_____

I am _____ years old

My favourite book is _____

My favourite song is _____

My favourite word is _____

My favourite TV programme is _____

My favourite video/DVD is _____

This year, I have learned how to:

_____

_____

_____

Literacy for pre-school and nursery children

Some developments in the 3 to 4 years stage

Children of 3 or 4 no longer look like babies as their limbs lengthen and the round plumpness of their faces and bodies lessens. Now they are confident and agile movers who run, jump, skip, hop, climb and swing more often than they walk. As well as being whirlwinds of physical activity, they are becoming very sociable and enjoy friendships with adults outside the immediate family. Other carers, minders, teachers and early years professionals, as well as neighbours or shopkeepers, become important to them.

> *Marian was reminded recently of the widening social worlds of this age group when 4-year-old Dylan told her that his new best friend was George, the driver of the school bus, and George would have to have a Christmas present!*

But it is friendships with other children that really matter at this stage and begin to be so satisfying that pre-schoolers and nursery children will make huge efforts to play with other children, even if it means not being able to get their own way in every game or play activity. All this socialising with other children and adults calls for excellent communication, language and diplomacy skills and that is why going to a playgroup, nursery or kindergarten setting often gives a child's language development a huge boost. We might call this the age of the chatterbox as 3 and 4-year-olds can be great little conversationalists, often talking non-stop to people, animals, books and toys, as well as to themselves. They can speak at great length now because they've hit on the trick of using 'and' to link lots and lots of clauses. All the negative words like 'no', 'not' and 'never' are used by children of this age as they assert their independence and determination! They also begin to ask for explanations about everything they see, hear and find, so parents, early childhood professionals, and other adults are bombarded with 'why', 'why', 'why' as they try to answer the questions children ask.

One other characteristic of most children in this age group is the rich imaginative life they lead. This is obvious when we hear them talking to toys and objects, making up wildly exciting games with other children – often involving lots of chasing, jumping and super heroes – or experiencing frightening dreams. Perhaps we should call this the age of the dressing-up box, when a few hats, scarves and drapes turn the child into any character from a story or a TV cartoon.

4.1 Dylan, 4 years, in his Superman cape

By the time they are 3 years of age many children, particularly in the developed countries of the world, are attending day care centres, pre-schools, playgroups, kindergartens, or nursery schools and classes. There are lots of misunderstandings about what goes on in these early years settings, or what ought to go on. The kinds of questions often asked by parents, grandparents, or other members of the community, reflect the widespread confusion about how best to develop early literacy with 3 to 4-year-olds. Three typical questions about pre-school learning, writing and reading are:

- Do children learn anything in pre-schools and nurseries, apart from sharing and getting on with other people?
- Shouldn't they be sitting down and learning their letters and sounds?
- When will they be ready for proper reading books?

We will take a look at each of these three questions and make some positive suggestions for supporting young children's literacy development.

Question 1: **Do children learn anything in pre-schools and nurseries, apart from sharing and getting on with other people?**

First, we need to be quite clear that there is nothing trivial about learning to share and get along with other children and adults. The social and emotional development of children is crucial to their lifelong health and well-being and makes it possible for them to learn successfully. This aspect of development is so important that countries as far apart as England and New Zealand make it a required part of the early years curriculum.

Second, it is obvious that children have certain inborn tendencies and temperaments and in the early years of care and education there are great opportunities for families and professionals to encourage and strengthen the kinds of dispositions that will help young children to learn successfully all through their lives. Many nursery settings in Europe, Australia, New Zealand and the USA plan their work with the children in order to support

47

dispositions such as curiosity, persistence, co-operation, playfulness and love of learning.

Third, we need to understand that a lot is known about how young children learn and this can be summed up quite simply:

Young children learn most successfully through play, communication and talk, and hands-on experiences.

These are what we might like to call the roots of learning and all the other 'academic' things that people suggest cannot be learned in pre-schools and nurseries are actually flourishing in those settings that value children's play, languages and active learning. If you work with young children or care for them at home, try to see the literacy, mathematics, science, history, geography, physical skills, creativity and cultural understandings in their play, talk and investigations.

Ask yourself what learning goes on at bath-time, on the beach, digging in the earth, unpacking the shopping, baking cookies, talking to grandma, playing cards, painting the fence, putting the wooden blocks away, banging saucepan lids – or wearing them as hats?

You will find it easier to identify the different kinds of learning if you make a few notes as you observe the children.

Play is a special way of exploring all kinds of possibilities and even taking big risks in a very safe context. So, as they pretend to be chased by monsters, or hide from lions, young children enjoy a small taste of fear and plan a few useful strategies for escaping the dangers they have invented. When they change roles and become the frightening shark themselves, they experience life from the other side. It's a bit like trying on a mask or a costume in order to become someone else. Children often pretend to be other people they know such as parents and teachers, or the characters from stories, or even machines like vacuum cleaners and windscreen wipers! They seem to be asking, 'what does it feel like to be someone or something else?'

All this imaginary activity helps children make sense of the world and the powerful feelings they have about people and what happens to them. It is also the best possible preparation for understanding stories and picture books and getting ready for reading. The oral stories we tell and the stories printed in books are ways of playing and pretending too and if we don't value

4.2 Clair in her shark towel

children's play in the early years we are not helping them to become confident storytellers and readers.

Hands-on experiences are a reminder that children's earliest learning is done by being as physically active as possible: moving, touching, tasting, shaking, bashing and taking things apart. In the first year of life all this activity actually builds the thinking connections in the brain and once toddlers are on the move they continue to develop their ability to think by:

- exploring their environment;
- doing things with people;
- playing with toys and other objects.

As they reach the 3s and 4s stage young children develop some special ways of thinking and these are known as **schemas**. You will probably recognise these if you think about the striking obsessions some children have with, for example, putting things in bags, hiding themselves in cupboards or under blankets, or painting or scribbling all over their finished pictures. This is an enveloping, or covering up, schema and is probably a way of thinking about how things and people appear and disappear. Other children are always busy moving things from one place to another in their homes and nurseries, carrying huge bags of toys and objects around with them, or wheeling carts and buggies full of luggage around. This is known as a transporting schema and it obviously helps children to think about the nature of movement and locations – a great starter for physics and geography!

In the mornings Mattias likes to gather up pyjamas from all the beds and take them off to a big couch where he sits and silently passes them from one side of his body to the other.

There are many other schemas. If you want to know more see the references at the end of the chapter.

In the pre-school years children do spend a lot of time drawing, painting, sticking and pasting, playing with sand, mud, water, sticks, stones and leaves, or moulding clay, dough and other 'soft stuff'. These creations are changed and altered as the child goes along and can be anything the child wishes. They too are active ways of thinking about, or **representing**, what the child has seen, heard, enjoyed or even worried about. Once again we see that in order to think about experiences and make sense of the world children must be doing things. They also need lots of opportunities to explore interesting places, indoors and outdoors. This is why children's environments are often called an important extra 'teacher' by early years experts.

Talk and communication, including the sign languages used by the hearing impaired, usually go hand in hand with children's active thinking. But the company of caring and interested adults to talk to raises children's learning to a higher level. Indeed, it has been known for years that children can learn surprisingly complex things in partnership with an interested adult who helps but doesn't take over. Children actually think beyond their apparent abilities when doing it alongside an expert. How many pre-schoolers have surprised you with their knowledge of car maintenance, videos, cell phones and computers, chicken farming or languages other than English? Surely they've learnt these things with an expert adult or older child.

Talk in any language enables children to:

- communicate with other people and express their own needs and feelings;
- sort out their own ideas;
- share their ideas, feelings and interests;
- reflect on past experiences and make sense of them;

- sort out new experiences and link them to things they already know;
- enjoy the sounds of languages and play with rhymes and rhythms;
- realise gradually that what people say is often written down as signs, messages and notices.

At this point we are talking directly about early literacy and our second question has to be tackled.

Question 2: Shouldn't they be sitting down and learning their letters and sounds?

'No' is the short answer!

Literacy learning starts well before teachers sit children down to learn letters and sounds. In fact, there is a very real danger for young children that too much sitting down and filling in worksheets can undermine literacy learning and positive dispositions towards literacy. Literacy is experienced daily by very young children who are on the move, out and about, living in their communities.

Young children love to make marks on any damp surface and they will draw and 'write' with anything that leaves a mark: water, food, lipstick, shaving foam, or even pencils and crayons. This love of making marks soon links up with the fact that

4.3 Dylan, 3 years 6 months, drawing in the sand

children live in homes and neighbourhoods that are swamped in print and pictures. Print is everywhere and people can be found doing writing nearly everywhere, including producing 'text' from a range of electronic gadgets.

So, young children have:

- a powerful desire to make marks;
- examples of all kinds of print around them;
- plenty of opportunities to watch older children and adults writing and printing.

What then can families and early years professionals do to encourage and develop 3 and 4-year-old children's interest in marks and print?

- We can make sure that children have the materials for mark making and writing:
  - all kinds of markers and papers of different colours and textures;
  - paints of varied thickness and brushes of different sizes;
  - chalks for chalk boards and outside hard surfaces;
  - sheets of paper to pin on walls or easels for vertical writing – like graffiti!
  - finger paints; dough; damp sand; mud; water to mark dry walls, fences and paths;
  - simple clipboards for writing while 'on the move'.

- We can make sure that children see other people reading and writing:
  - We have to make sure that we are writing and reading alongside the children.
  - We can let the children help us write our own lists, letters and messages, perhaps by adding their drawings, scribbles, names and kisses to them.
  - We can talk out loud about what we are doing when we are engaging in everyday literacy experiences such as looking up a telephone number, writing a note to a parent, reading a recipe and so on.
  - We need to let the 3s and 4s see as many older children and adults as possible writing, drawing, text messaging and word processing.

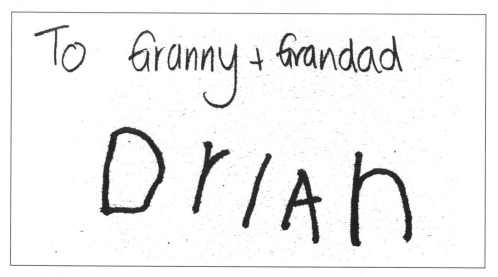

4.4 Dylan, just 5, writes his name on a note to his grandparents

- We can create special places, indoors and outside, where children can find all the materials they need for drawing, mark making and writing.

See the end of the chapter for some notes on 'Setting up a writing area' and 'Literacy out-of-doors'.

- We can bring into our homes and early years settings plenty of the everyday print that we use in our communities and workplaces. This means anything, from carrier bags, newspapers and calendars, to catalogues, recipes and official forms! Early years settings can also 'flood' their dramatic play areas with appropriate print and writing materials.

Print in the play house or home area
- cookery books
- recipe cards
- pens
- pencils
- scrap paper
- calendars
- diaries
- newspapers
- comics
- letters

- junk mail
- telephone books and message pads
- catalogues
- maps and guide books
- children's books
- magazines
- TV guides
- food packages
- cans
- carrier bags
- computer keyboard
- dressing up clothes with labels and logos
- car users' manuals
- instruction books for household equipment

and so on.

Other print-rich dramatic play areas
- market stall/village store/supermarket/bakers;
- office/estate agent (realtor)/travel agent, post office;
- restaurants and 'take-away' – pizza, Indian, Chinese, coffee bar;
- fire station, lifeboat station, library;
- hospital, baby clinic, doctor's surgery, veterinarian's surgery;
- hairdresser, repair garage, petrol (filling) station, building/construction site.

Literacy for real

All this exposure to printed materials will inspire children to want to become real writers and readers. Their curiosity about what goes on in the world and what grown-ups and big kids do with print will also drive them to ask:

- What does this print 'say'?
- What is it for?
- How do you do it?

Meaningful print from the real world is the best possible material for introducing young children to:

- letter names and some of their usual sounds;
- the initial sounds of favourite names, places, foods and activities;
- the enjoyable and amusing rhymes that they hear when words start or end with similar letters.

Some ideas for activities that turn children into writers and readers

- Collecting and playing with 'everyday print' – packaging, brochures, newsprint, etc.
- Going on print-discovery walks – looking at signs, advertisements, numbers, shopping malls and community centres, etc.
- Shopping for ingredients, cooking and eating – using recipes, menus, food packets, shopping lists, bills and receipts.
- Making puppets and performing plays and concerts – with scripts, tickets, publicity posters and programmes.
- Making, writing and posting – greetings cards (seasonal, birthday, get well), letters (invitations to visitors, thank-you to visitors, keeping in touch with absent children, parents, etc).
- Making lists – things to do, favourite foods/toys/videos/activities/games/software.
- Making post boxes – for the children's birthday cards, for greetings, for all the festivals the children and their communities celebrate.
- Making badges (buttons) to wear – with names, pictures, messages.
- Making posters – about favourite books, visits, pets, sports, games.
- Writing their own names – 'signing in' daily on a sheet of paper, or in a big book, or on a chalkboard.
- Filling in forms – from post offices, shops, clinics, magazines, government offices.
- Making simple books – folded, stapled or sewn sheets of paper; fill with children's drawings, photos, cut-out pictures, little stories, personal news, rhymes, songs, poems. Write for the children – to their dictation – as well as encouraging them to 'have a go'.
- Communicating – set up a notice board for press cuttings, photos, messages, accounts of what the children are doing, future plans for the curriculum, local news and community events (involve the children's families).

Question 3: When will they be ready for proper reading books?

It all depends on what you mean by proper reading books. If you are thinking about the reading scheme books or primers (like Janet and John or Dick and Dora), then we must say that they have no useful place in the early reading experiences of children under 5. However, if you really do mean proper books written and illustrated by serious authors and artists with a story to tell and genuine insight into the lives and feelings of young children, then the children are 'ready' from birth. As Chapter 2 explained, infants are never too young to start sharing books with caring adults and older children. Early reading has to be a mutually satisfying partnership and this should still be continuing as children reach their third and fourth years. At this stage we can pick out some important features of early reading:

- sharing the pleasure;
- collecting and reading quality books;
- using story props.

Sharing the pleasure

In the early days of sharing books the child needs an older and wiser partner who takes on a lot of the reading task but still leaves room for the child to chip in with a giggle, an offer to turn the page, a sound effect, the name of a character, joining in with a chorus or repeated refrain, and even asking a difficult question, such as 'Where's their mummy gone?'

Reading the pictures and constructing a story from them is one of the earliest and cleverest things very young readers do. Adults can help by encouraging children to scan the pictures, talk about what is going on, ask a few useful questions: 'What do you think will happen if the pig gets in the boat?' Asking young readers to predict what might come next is a useful strategy. Good readers of any age are always good predictors of what will come next. But don't over-do it with young readers and turn every page into a terrible quiz!

Successful early reading depends on lots of enjoyable re-reading of favourite books and you will tire of the umpteenth reading of

Mr Gumpy's Outing long before the children do, but keep going, because repetition is essential if children are to get the text in their minds. Matching the sounds of the words with the familiar meanings and the look of the words is essential in reading. The familiar voice of a teacher, parent or carer reading from a book brings print to life for children and teaches more about phonics (the sounds of letters or groups of letters) than any number of phonic programmes and workbooks.

Close looks at interesting words and chunks of print are possible when adults share books with individual children and very small groups, or use some of the books now available in a 'big book' size. Show the children the really important words like the names of characters, or words that pack an emotional punch like 'sad', 'angry', 'wild thing', 'bump'. Pick out some initial words and sounds that occur in their own names; get them to join in all the repeated phrases and verses in story and rhyme books; draw their attention to rhyming words and get them to think up more words that rhyme.

A collection of quality books

It is essential that children have easy access to a collection of quality books. It does not have to be very large but it should have a varied range and include old favourites that fall apart with loving use, as well as new books borrowed from libraries or bought for the children's collection. We have provided a list of books for a 'Starter Collection' in Useful Resources (Chapter 7) and there is a note on setting up a book area at the end of this chapter. These are books that many children, families and early years educators find enjoyable, but you also need to collect your own favourites and follow your children's interests. Just try to include books from some of the following categories:

- traditional tales, myths and legends;
- picture books, lift-the-flap books, books for bath and buggy;
- rhymes and poetry;
- animal stories;
- family stories;
- emotional and moral issues;
- non-fiction or factual books.

Using story props

Children of 3 and 4 years are 'hands on' in their approach to most things and the excitement of reading can be shared and increased if we take advantage of all the story tapes, toys and play materials that teachers call 'story props'.

Audio tapes

Audio tapes of many children's books are now widely available and they are very popular with children and their families. Listening to the tape of a familiar book helps children to learn a story and match the sounds they hear to the words on the page. It can also be a very comforting and private experience to listen to a taped story in bed, in a quiet nursery corner, or on a long journey. There are increasing numbers of video taped versions of children's books being produced and these provide a lovely focus for sharing TV viewing and talking about what has been seen. And it is still great to go back to the book and have an even stronger grasp of the storyline and the text. Parents and professionals can build on the children's enthusiasm for audio tapes by making their own tapes of themselves telling stories, singing songs and rhymes and reading favourite books. There is something very special about hearing a familiar and loved voice reading and singing on tape.

Play materials

Play materials based on a traditional story or a children's book can also be made by parents and early years educators. The simplest approach is a set of cut-out drawings of the main characters, backed with velcro or magnetic tape so that they can be moved about on a metal or fabric-covered board – or a fridge door, filing cabinet or carpet! As they play with these cut-outs children can remember and re-tell the story.

Toy props

A toy prop is a delightful addition to any story telling or book reading session. It is possible to get hold of a soft toy dog that looks just like *Spot*, or a little toy *Daisy* duck, or find a favourite teddy bear that can stand in for *Little Bear*. The special thing about these toys is the fact that a child can tell the story to them and take on the role of the older and wiser reading partner! We can probably all think of lots of other ways of bringing stories to life for our children by using objects that are really important in the tale. What about wooden spoons and bowls for Goldilocks, a soup ladle and big pot for Pumpkin Soup, or straw, sticks and bricks for 'the three little pigs'?

Storysacks

Storysacks are an exciting way of making and using storyprops regularly in early years settings, as well as in the children's homes and communities. They can be made for the setting as a joint effort between families and professional early years workers. They can also be taken home to use, just like library books.

A storysack is a large cloth bag containing a good quality young child's picture book with supporting materials (Griffiths, 1997, p.2).

These materials are an appropriate soft toy, or doll, or puppet, to represent the main character, and maybe some objects that feature in the story. There is usually a non-fiction book that links with the picture book's theme in some way and a taped version of the story. For older children, related language and maths games can be added to the sack, as well as a card of suggestions to help families develop some listening, reading and writing activities around the book.

A literacy snapshot

By now, children can decide on all of the information recorded in the snapshot, and most will want to do some of the writing.

My literacy snapshot

This is a picture of me.

My name is _____

I am doing what I like to do best _____

I am _____ years old.

My favourite book is _____

My favourite song is _____

My favourite TV programme is _____

My favourite video/DVD is _____

This year, I have learned how to:

_____

_____

_____

More about schemas

Nutbrown, C. (1999) *Threads of Thinking. Young Children Learning and the Role of Early Education* (2nd edition). London: Paul Chapman Publishing.

Whalley, M. and Pen Green Centre Team (2001) *Involving Parents in their Children's Learning*. London: Paul Chapman Publishing.

Setting up a writing area

A special place for writing: a corner; a table or two; a low shelf unit plus table.

Choose a quiet area away from doors, pathways, blockplay and role-play. It can be close to the book area.

Provide all kinds of crayons, felt pens, pencils, biros, erasers, pencil sharpeners, etc.

Provide paper of all kinds: unlined, lined, coloured, computer print-outs, forms, diaries, notebooks, writing pads and envelopes, airmail letters, message pads and shopping lists.

Include some maps, street directories, phone books and early dictionaries and alphabet books.

Printing sets, typewriters, paper clips and sticky tape for making books are useful.

Perhaps the computer, if you have one, should be in this area. Do you have word and picture keyboard overlays, and simple instruction cards of drawings to show how to use the equipment?

Literacy out-of-doors

Set up a mark-making and writing trolley to store and move markers and papers outside.

Find a small trolley or wheeled basket to store and transport books, maps, guides, etc outside.

Provide clipboards and pencils so that children can write anywhere outside.

Make and laminate notices and children's name cards for the outside – who is here today; what we are growing; where to park the bikes, scooters, prams and buggies; games we like to play; notices for parents; birthday greetings to children and staff.

Set aside walls and/or hard ground surfaces for chalking and water painting.

Put magnetic boards and magnetic letters and numerals outside (store on the literacy trolley).

Provide laminated sets of instructions on how to play popular group games with the children (to help parents and workers).

Provide cushions, blankets, wind breaks, big umbrellas and parasols for cosy, sheltered reading areas and dens.

Paint or chalk road layouts, make laminated road signs and instructions to give purpose and order to wheeled vehicle play.

Create an area with all the signs and literacy materials for a pretend fire station, garage, motorway service area, accident and emergency hospital, bus station.

Make little boxes, pigeon-holes, or post boxes, so that the children and the staff can leave messages and letters for each other.

Setting up a book area

Screen the area off from messy or boisterous play.

Try to find a carpeted area; it also needs floor cushions and/ or soft seats, curtains, a low table for plants and flowers, or a shelf to display collections of shells, pebbles, seeds, wood etc.

Put some pictures and posters about books on the walls and some photos of the children enjoying books and reading.

Books should be on low shelves, tables or in baskets.

Try hard to display the beautiful covers of picture books, or open a few at stunning illustrations.

Keep the collection small and change it frequently – but a core collection of real favourites should always be available.

Always display prominently in this area the books that you have been reading to the children so that they can look at them for themselves.

Have some storysacks in this area, as well as other story props you have collected – stored in attractive baskets and boxes.

Keep a cassette recorder with headphones and tapes in the book area.

5

Literacy for children in transition to school

Introduction

School entry is usually a mixture of stress and anxiety, excitement and anticipation. The curriculum moves from a more or less equal focus on all areas of development – social, emotional, cognitive and physical – to a primary focus on cognitive development. There is more emphasis on comparing children with other children rather than focusing on their own individual progress. There are fewer staff members in relation to the number of children in a class. Playgrounds can be large and intimidating. If they've been in a multi-age setting, the children are used to being the oldest and most competent. At school, they're the youngest and least experienced. Both parents and early childhood educators want to do their best to prepare children for the school experience, but well-meaning efforts may place additional stress on children rather than building their sense of competence and confidence.

In many countries, children start school between the ages of 5 and 6 years, although the range overall can be from 3 to 7. It is increasingly common for governments to support at least one year of pre-school education prior to school entry. Educators working with children in the year prior to school entry will, almost certainly, be working with children who have had a very wide range of early literacy experiences, and who are demonstrating very different understandings, skills and dispositions. For example:

5.1 Syoun does her homework for Chinese School

- Some children may already be reading and writing and be competent users of technology such as computers and videos.
- Some children will have been in various forms of long day care since they were babies. Their literacy experiences may have been encountered primarily in group care. If the staff in those settings did not support early literacy, or if they adopted an inappropriately formal and academic approach to teaching early literacy, the children may have limited concepts of print and may have developed negative dispositions towards literacy.
- Some children will have had very rich literacy experiences in their homes, but in a language other than English. When they start school, they may find themselves in an English-only environment for the first time.
- Some children will have had rich, complementary literacy experiences at home and in early childhood settings for five or six years, but may enter schools in which the expectations of teaching and learning are very different from those they have experienced prior to school entry.

This makes the task of supporting children's early literacy in the transition between prior to school settings and the first year of school a very challenging one.

Many children attend more than one early childhood setting before they start school. For example, they may be in long day care two days a week because their parents are working. They may also attend two or three mornings of pre-school because the parents want them to 'get ready for school'. Their experiences in these settings may be quite different. In one, the educators may believe that literacy should be left alone until it is taught at school, and that, beyond reading stories to groups of children, there is no need for them to include an explicit focus on literacy in prior to school settings. In another setting, there may be a strong literacy programme based on literacy-enriched play and authentic literacy experiences.

When children start school, they enter yet another setting and one in which there may be many new adjustments needed. At school, the pressures of external assessments and official curriculum documents, combined with large classes, may mean that the literacy teaching children encounter is more formal and academic than they are used to. Play-based learning may disappear or be reduced to something children do in their spare time, after they've finished their 'proper work'.

Differences between prior to school settings and the first years of school appear to have become greater over the past few years. In part, this seems to have resulted from concerns about literacy levels. The differences in teaching practices and classroom organisation can be so great that one would think that children change dramatically over the holidays that precede school entry. We need to remember that a 5 or 6-year-old child is the same child, whether he is in day care, nursery, preschool or the first year of school. In all cases children's learning experiences must match with their individual abilities and interests and must support positive dispositions towards literacy learning.

So, what can educators do to help children in the transition to school? In this chapter we discuss three key areas that should be integral to the literacy experiences of children in all of the settings mentioned. The three we have chosen are:

- literacy-enriched play;
- the importance of observing and building upon individual differences in literacy learning;
- partnerships between families and educators in supporting children's early literacy.

Literacy-enriched play

Probably the greatest area of concern in the minds of teachers, parents and children when children are in the period of transition to school is whether or not the children will be successful in learning to read and write, so that is the main focus we will take in this chapter. It is important to remember that learning to read and write is supported by many activities apart from formal teaching and learning. Children between 4 and 6 learn through play, especially role play, which offers many opportunities to talk and listen, sing and chant, take on different roles, tell stories, and generally explore the functions and tools of literacy.

Playing 'schools'

A school role play centre, with uniforms, boxes of names, books such as children's dictionaries, an alphabet frieze, exercise books, and so on, is usually very popular with children in the year before they enter school. They enjoy 'playing schools', although many educators are somewhat taken aback by the children's mimicry of their intonations and expressions, especially in moments of impatience.

A centre set up as a classroom can be linked with a publishing centre for books made by the children. The written text can be dictated by the children or copied by them from adult writing. Some children may be ready to write some words themselves. Others may write words and then ask an adult to write them in 'grown up writing'. All children need many opportunities to recognise and write their name.

Educators can join in children's play in ways that give them opportunities to rehearse some of the knowledge that they need when they start school, such as their full name, their telephone number, and their address; whether they have siblings in the school and what their parents' names are.

The school activity centre should also include many of the educational games with rules that are common in early years classrooms. Children enjoy playing simple card games, lotto of various types, bingo and the first versions of various adult word games, such as Pictionary or Scrabble. They may change the rules to suit themselves, and there is often much debate about what is allowed and what isn't. Rules can be written or read. Letters or words can be linked with pictures, as children play with sounds.

Popular culture

Often, children's play reflects popular culture, for example, superheroes from television. This often disturbs educators, who are concerned about the violence or the gender bias or the racism that may be evident in some programmes. However, when we think about some of the old fairy tales, or the stories of Hans Anderson and the folk tales collected by the Grimm brothers, we realise that violence, gender bias and racism are not confined to television! Play offers children a way of working through emotions in a safe situation and can be a stimulus to many positive literacy activities. Jackie Marsh (1999), in the UK, has done some very interesting work with young children, building on their interests in popular culture, in the belief that children become actively and enthusiastically involved in literacy when their interests are harnessed. For example, using the Teletubbies as the focus, Marsh made 'tubby custard' with the children, who each had a copy of the recipe. Later, they were encouraged to write their own recipes for Teletubby toast and visited the Teletubby website.

However, not all children find that their interest in popular culture is supported when they reach school. Simon was a very keen Pokémon fan. He drew very detailed pictures of Pokémon figures and was a leader in many involved games at pre-school. At the first school assembly, he was devastated to hear the Principal announce that Pokémon was banned from the school. The Principal's concerns had arisen because of incidents of envy and theft the previous year, but Simon took it as a personal criticism of what was his passion.

Problem-solving

Because they are starting to be able to think about how things may affect other people, children's play can extend their thinking and talking, as well as offering opportunities for reading and writing. There is often more potential than educators realise to extend the play that occurs in such socio-dramatic play centres. For example, it is common for classrooms to include a restaurant as a focus for socio-dramatic play. Caroline Barratt-Pugh (2002) gives an interesting account of how she worked to extend children's social awareness of literacy by setting problems for the children to solve. The central problem involved a mother wanting to bring her 20-month-old twins to the restaurant. Issues of access, high chairs, appropriate food, changing facilities, a safe place to put the stroller, all engaged the children in active thinking and problem solving, as well as extending their literacy understandings.

Observing and building upon individual differences in literacy learning

Children show a great deal of knowledge about reading and writing in the stages leading up to their becoming conventional readers and writers. Their demonstrations of this knowledge are often referred to as 'emergent' reading and writing (Teale and Sulzby, 1986; Sulzby, 1985, 1994).

Children of this age often read to themselves or their friends or their toys. They also enjoy writing signs and lists and stories and letters and birthday cards, either on paper or using a computer. Adults may call this 'pretend' reading or writing, and add, 'Well, they're not *really* reading [or writing], are they?' It is true that most young children at this stage are not reading or writing conventionally. However, their emergent reading and writing can show us many things about what they know and are able to do.

Emergent writing

Let's look briefly at writing. Children start making marks at a very early age, if they are given opportunities to do so. First of all, they make random marks – dots and lines. As they gain some control over the marker, they make more controlled marks like circles and spirals. If their attention has been drawn regularly to how writing is used in their everyday lives, they will start to write in appropriate patterns, even though there will, at first, be no

26/11/01
Grandad with his beard

5.2 Clair's picture with letter-like shapes

recognisable words. You may notice, for example, that their shopping lists look different from their stories in the way the marks are arranged on the page.

At some point between the ages of 3 and 5, they understand that there is a difference between drawing and writing. At this stage, some forms may appear that look rather like letters even though they are not named as such. Clair (see picture 5.2) included

Day 7: Friday
• At home with Sally

• We made masks

• I made puppets with shadows for Callum but he took the torch

5.3 Lily's holiday

the three forms seen in her picture as part of most of her pictures for several weeks. She knew that they were 'writing' and would tell anyone who asked what the writing said. These same letter-like forms could say many different things, according to the drawing, but she always identified them as writing, rather than drawing.

The first word children learn to read and write is often their name. Children with access to a computer will often be able to write their name on a computer before they can write it with a marker, since it is easier to simply press a key than to have the fine motor control to write each letter. With encouragement, they will begin to experiment with writing more and more. Lily's family encouraged her to keep a diary when they went on holidays (see picture 5.3).

Especially in the first years of school, children are encouraged to write more and more. They may do stencils and worksheets, write sentences to go with pictures, write short stories or directions or make class-made books about excursions. Be careful not to push too hard. One child said, during a school excursion to the zoo, 'Don't notice anything. You'll have to write about it!'

As writing moves closer to the conventional, children start to use what is often called 'invented spelling'. This is an important stage in their understanding, because it shows that they know that there is a relationship between talking and writing, and between sounds and letters. Beginning sounds come first, then final sounds, and later middle sounds, especially if these sounds are vowel sounds. 'Book', for example, may be written as 'bk'.

The children learn about repeated patterns, and how you can write many words once you know one. Books like Dr Seuss's *The Cat in the Hat* are loved by many children at this stage. Children learn to write, as they learn most things, when they are in a supportive environment that encourages them to explore, offers them opportunities to see writing modelled, provides interaction with adults who are ready to help them take the next step at the right time and which presents interesting challenges.

Emergent reading

Reading and writing develop together and are closely linked in terms of children's understandings. Young children usually enjoy reading to adults if they are invited to do so. However, they will only be happy to do this if they have a good relationship with the adult and do not feel anxious or under pressure. It sometimes helps to say something like, 'Read it your own way. It doesn't have to be like grown up reading.' Some of the things you will learn from engaging with a child in an emergent reading session are these:

- **Book-handling skills**. Does the child hold the book appropriately, open it at the right place, start at the beginning and turn the pages one by one? In English, this means holding the book with its spine on the child's left. The pages will be turned from right to left.

  It is important to remember, however, that not all languages are written the same way. A young Arabic boy was reprimanded by the teacher because, 'He always looks at the ending first'. He did not need reprimanding. He needed to be shown the difference between where a book starts in English and where it starts in Arabic. The teacher needed more understanding of the child's home literacy experiences and of the conventions of written Arabic.

- **Eye movements**. Is the child reading by looking at the pictures or by following the words? Perhaps she is doing both, using the pictures to help her with words she is not sure of.

- **Sense of story**. As the child progresses through the story, is there a story line, or is the child labelling each picture separately? If there is a storyline, how complete is it? Does it have a beginning, middle and end? If so, how close are these to the written text?

- **Book language**. Is the child beginning to include 'book language' such as 'he said' or 'she whispered'? You may also notice the child using words that are not commonly used in everyday life, but that are included in books. For example, one sentence in *The Tale of Peter Rabbit* says, in part, ... *some friendly sparrows ... flew to him in great excitement, and implored him to exert himself.*

  Sentences, too, may be formed differently than they are in everyday life, and the child's emergent reading may reflect this. For example, a sentence in *Owl Babies* says, *Soft and silent, she swooped through the trees to Sarah and Percy and Bill.*

- **Intonation.** Partly because of the language used, and partly because of the tradition of oral storytelling, reading and talking do not sound the same. When the child is doing an emergent reading, does his tone of voice sound like reading or talking, or is it a mixture of both?

- **Conventional reading/decoding.** If the child is beginning to read conventionally, how is this done? For example, does she read some of the words and fill in the words she doesn't know with words that make sense in terms of the story? Is she trying

to sound out unfamiliar words, or is she reading some words
and leaving out others?

Once you have a good idea of what children already know, you
can help them extend their learning. They may need more
opportunities to handle books. The older children get, the more
likely it is that their experiences of book reading are in groups,
with the teacher holding the book so that all the children can see
the pictures. If children are to be given opportunities to hold the
book and turn the pages, reading sessions must be conducted
often with individuals and small groups of two or three, not
always with large groups or whole classes. Literacy play can also
help develop book-handling skills. Make sure that there are story
books by the doll's cot, recipe books in the home corner kitchen,
magazines in the doctor's waiting room and so on.

One of the best ways to develop a sense of story is to offer
children many chances both to hear stories and to tell them.
Children are encouraged to tell stories when there are puppets and
a puppet theatre, felt board figures and a felt board, masks and
hats to wear and when drama is part of their curriculum. Class-
made books can be based on children's retellings of incidents that
have made an impression on them. Excursions outside the pre-
school or school setting usually provide lots of exciting inspiration,
like a lost packed lunch or a trip on an underground train.
Children can also make up new versions of known stories. Talking
about stories and how they are structured is another way of
drawing children's attention to their structure. This is a good
inclusion when they are developing their own stories for class-
made books. 'How will this story start? What will happen next?
What was the problem? How will it be solved?'

Book language and intonation develop through much practice
and discussion. Reading is not simply a matter of decoding marks
on paper, although, of course, children must be able to decode in
order to be able to read unfamiliar texts. It is always depressing to
hear young readers stumble through a boring text with no
expression or interest. One child in his first year of school was
quite a fluent and expressive conventional reader. His mother was
astounded, a few weeks after he began school, to have him come
home and read painfully and slowly, word by word, a text that
was well below his reading ability. When she asked him why he
was reading that way, he said, 'Well, that's the way we read at

school.' The wonder and excitement of well-written books must be an integral part of every reading curriculum. Acting out stories or reading in parts, with a narrator, encourages intonation that engages the listener as well as giving pleasure to the reader or actor.

Children often start focusing on words through learning the way their own name looks when it's written down, and through recognising familiar signs and logos in the community. Once children are noticing some letters and words, they can be encouraged to notice more. Many games and activities will extend children's attention to written text. 'Let's see how many words we can find in this book that start with the same letter as your name.' 'How many words can we think of that rhyme with Sam? Let's write them all down.' 'How many signs are in our playground?' 'We'd better make a sign for our classroom door.' 'Let's make our voices sound like each of these words: delighted, angry, loud, soft, questioning, commanding, frightened.' 'Who knows a very long word? What about a very short one? One with three syllables?' An interest in and an enjoyment of language is one of the pillars of successful literacy.

Building partnerships between families and educators in the transition to school literacy

Many early childhood settings, whether pre-school, day care, nursery, or first year of school, now have transition programmes in place to help children and families become used to the new location and ways of doing things. Sometimes, the transition programme includes a literacy perspective. For example, when Clair visited her new school at the end of her pre-school year, a photo was taken of each child when they first arrived. By the time they left, they each had a badge to wear that had their photo, name and the name of the school. It was the upper primary children who had made the badges. Clair wore hers very proudly.

It is important to make sure that the transition period is one that supports children's confidence and self-esteem. Sometimes, however, perceived pressures to 'get the children ready for school' can result in staff introducing inappropriate practices in pre-schools and day care centres. This is sometimes called 'the push-down curriculum'. This means that prior to school programmes become more and more like traditional formal schooling and put pressure on children to engage with developmentally inappropriate formal academic tasks such as tracing or reading flash cards or learning de-contextualised letter-sound relationships. An important part of successful transition in literacy is development of a strategy to increase shared understandings between families, early years teachers and prior to school staff about key practices that support early literacy. This can happen through informal visits, planned exchanges of information, shared portfolios of children's work, parent meetings, newsletters and so on.

Generally speaking, in prior to school settings, the focus is on developing children's awareness of the social practices of literacy, making sure they have positive dispositions to literacy and involving them in literacy-enriched play. This emphasis is very important. Sometimes, parents may worry that there is not enough focus on word level skills. One parent complained, 'I don't know whether Maria knows the other letters. She doesn't know her last name...she has a last name as well and she can't do that because they are not teaching her any other letters... There are millions of other things to write, as well as just her name.' It is absolutely crucial that early years practitioners respond in positive and supportive ways to these kinds of concerns expressed by parents. We do have a responsibility to stick to our principles, but we must also be able to explain simply the knowledge about language and literacy development that our principles and practices are based on. The fears of parents are genuine because they know that their children's lives will be restricted and damaged if they fail to become literate adults. We have to convince families that our literacy priorities are the appropriate ones and that pushing isolated word-level skills too soon can result in anxious, de-skilled and de-motivated children.

We have referred to sharing information about literacy between families and educators. In the year prior to school, every effort should be made to extend this partnership to include teachers in the first year of school, school teachers in charge of transition programmes and school management. When a pre-school is part of a school, the process of exchanging information is, at least at a structural level, relatively straightforward. However, when children from one day care centre may be going to six or seven different primary schools, the process is much more difficult. Nevertheless, it can be done if there is a willingness in all parties to put in the

5.4 Visual discrimination and pattern making support early literacy learning

effort. Some helpful practices include exchanges of staff, shared professional development activities, visits by older children who will act as mentors in the first year of school, and social functions after hours, which bring together families, school teachers and prior to school educators.

There are many studies that confirm the importance of high quality, developmentally appropriate early childhood programmes. Early childhood educators have a fine line to walk between helping children get ready for school and standing up for what they know will be most helpful in this regard, which is, in our opinion, sending children to school with a love of and an interest in language, a knowledge of songs, stories and rhymes, an awareness of the many uses of literacy in their homes and communities and a positive disposition towards literacy learning.

There is a worrying emphasis in the current educational climate, both in Australia and England, on a skill and drill approach with a strong belief in baseline assessment of skills and standardised testing of skills in early childhood. This can result in children

My mum and dad and
me went on a holiday and
we saw lots of things and
played in the swimming pool.

Riley (F)   16/2/99 (DOB)

5.5 Story by Riley

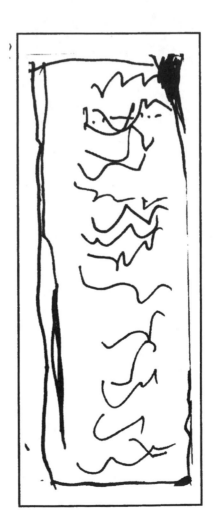

5.6 A list of names

feeling that they are failures at a very young age. Education should be about building children's confidence and positive dispositions towards learning as well as developing their abilities and understandings. Parents and early childhood educators who know this can work together to ensure that the transition to school literacy supports children's exploratory drive and sense of competence and confidence in themselves as learners. The practices we have described in this book are aimed at doing this. Perhaps one of the next steps to be taken is to encourage school principals, head teachers and policy makers to learn more about literacy practices in prior to school settings so that continuity in literacy learning develops through a 'push-up' curriculum instead of a 'push-down' curriculum.

A literacy snapshot

A literacy snapshot taken at the end of the year prior to school entry can be a wonderful memento for the family as well as a way of sharing information about the child's interests and abilities with his new teachers.

My literacy snapshot insert year

This is a picture of me.

My name is_____

I am _____ years old

My address is _____

My telephone number is _____

Next year I am going to school. My new school is _____
_____

My favourite book is _____

My favourite song is _____

My favourite TV programme is _____

My favourite video/DVD is _____

This year, I have learned how to:

_____

_____

_____

Let's think about ...

Play and literacy

Children learn through play. Babies use all their senses as they explore their surroundings and get to know their important people. They enjoy listening, watching, touching and being rocked, bounced and moved rhythmically. They respond to voices, faces, moving leaves, textures and sounds. These experiences are enjoyable and they are also ways of learning about language: the sounds of voices, rhythmic patterns, eye contacts and facial expressions.

Babies are also learning to expect things to happen again, as in care routines or games of peek-a-boo, and they are learning what they can do with their own bodies. This sounds a bit dull until we see the sheer excitement babies experience when we spin a mobile for them, play at hiding our faces behind blankets, or wiggle their toes and sing a rhyme. Babies' delight in physical play and language can be supported by bath-time water play, quiet times on their carers' laps with picture books, or investigating a 'treasure basket' that holds wooden and metal spoons, silky fabrics, shells, balls, lids, etc.

Toddlers are skilled at managing their own bodies and enjoy walking, running, jumping, hiding and climbing. They are also becoming great talkers, singers and dancers, and will start to use more than one language if they are growing up in bilingual families and communities. Toddlers frequently talk to themselves about what they are doing or what is happening and they talk to toys and even special objects like blankets.

They are learning how to talk about a wide range of events and ideas. They are beginning to use talk as a way of thinking and that is what is going on when they talk to themselves and even tell themselves what to do. Their play and talk with toys and objects shows us that they are developing the ability to imagine things and create their own pretend worlds. They are making up stories and laying the foundations for their own literacy. This sounds a bit grand and we have to remember that the toddlers are having a wonderful time and enjoying themselves!

The kinds of play activities that toddlers enjoy include setting up dens, camps or hiding places under tables, bushes and blankets, or in cupboards and big boxes. Here they can think and play imaginatively and also experience space and containment. Parks and wide-open spaces are essential for our all-action toddlers who need to run, swing, slide and spin round. But the walking and talking with their carers on these visits to parks and open areas can also be very stimulating for children's thinking and give them lots of new things to name, talk about, or draw, model and play at home. We can see the thinking of toddlers in so many of their favourite activities, such as playing with saucepans and lids, wrapping up toys in paper and laundry, packing things in baskets or bags, lining up models and small toys with great care, blowing and chasing bubbles. There are lots of mathematical and spatial ideas being explored, as well as emotional issues about people and things that appear and disappear. These same ideas are often in the books that toddlers enjoy and explain their love of 'lift the flaps' and very detailed pictures. They also want to be like the big folk and will really get into playing with newspapers, magazines and brochures.

Socio-dramatic play and literacy

Wanting to be like the big folk or like their favourite book or television character leads children into more and more socio-dramatic play, where they pretend to be someone or something else. Children can learn through socio-dramatic play what it is like to be a literate member of a society. Literacy is social practice. Think about when you go to a hospital, for example – there are signs to follow and forms to fill out everywhere you look. The receptionist may enter your details on a computer. As you wait for the doctor, you may read a magazine in the waiting room. If you have to be admitted, you may need to wear an identification bracelet. There will be a sign on the end of your bed, a temperature chart, x-rays and a cupboard that may be marked 'Medicines – poison'. Your friends may send you get well cards or books to read. All of these are the social practices of literacy that are part of being in a hospital.

So what does this mean in terms of children's play? It means that any area that is set up for socio-dramatic play should include appropriate resources that children can use to include literacy practices in their play. Whether they are the doctor, the nurse, the patient or the visitor, there will be literacy practices that are part of that role.

There are many socio-dramatic play activities that can be extended in this way, for example, a hairdresser's, shops of various sorts, a restaurant, a school classroom (particularly relevant for children who are going to start school the following year), a post office, a travel agent's, a construction site and so on.

Talking of construction sites, remember to include literacy resources in outdoor play. Cardboard and markers to make road signs, licence plates, building plans and so on make good additions to block or sand play.

Unfortunately, it seems particularly easy, in these days of increased pressure on raising literacy standards, to try to support children's early literacy learning in ways that are inappropriate for young children's learning. Some examples of what we consider to be inappropriate literacy activities for children before they start school are worksheets, flash cards, phonics drills of sounds not related to meaningful contexts and rote copying of words or letters. At this stage, it is more important to encourage them to deepen their understanding of how literacy works in society and they can do this best through incorporating literacy practices into their play.

The process works two ways. Excursions, books, videos and so on can inspire socio-dramatic play, then the play itself can be the basis for class-made books that include photographs of children or their drawings, and their stories or comments on the photos, the drawings, or their play experiences – who they were, how they felt, what they did and so on.

Of course, this doesn't mean that all of children's play involves them in role-playing real life. Much of their play is imaginative and creative, involving characters and scenarios that could never happen in real life, but are nonetheless real to them because of this. Children encounter imaginary characters and situations in fairy stories, myths and legends, science fiction, and action heroes in books, on video, on television, in comic books and so on. All of these types of literature, which are often called 'genres', can offer wonderful opportunities for children's creative self-expression.

Whether play is based in real life or in an imaginary world, it helps children to have resources they can use. Some settings use storysacks, which contain a book, puppets and other articles that let the child act out the story. Some settings have prop boxes and dressing-up clothes. All should have cardboard, paper and markers readily available to children. Felt boards and felt board figures, a big box to make into a theatre, craft materials to make masks – all of these stimulate children's imaginations and offer opportunities for creative play.

The adult's role in supporting literacy learning through play

It is important to think about the adult's role in children's play. It is sometimes tempting to turn children's play into a teaching opportunity, but we do not encourage this. One of the most important things about children's play is that it offers them opportunities to make up the rules, decide what the play is going to be, make choices about the directions the play will take and generally be in control of the activity. The adult can help by joining in the play – but only if they are invited or welcomed by the children, taking on a character role and using that role to model one or two appropriate literacy practices. For example, if the adult is a customer in a shop, he might take out a real or imaginary piece of paper and say, 'Now, let me see, what do I need? I've forgotten. Oh, yes, here it is. I wrote it down. I need some eggs to make a birthday cake.' Or, if the adult is a shop owner, she might say, 'Oh dear, I'm afraid we're out of shoes in that colour. Let me just look up the inventory and see if I've got any ordered.'

Summary

In summary, play that is literacy-enriched supports children's literacy in many ways:

• They extend their understanding about the many functions literacy plays in society.

- They develop and practise listening, speaking, emergent reading and writing.
- They have opportunities for creative and imaginative self-expression.
- They deepen and broaden their knowledge of the real world and of fantasy worlds.
- They can try out different roles and start to experience what it is like to be someone different in a different context.
- They learn to link what they read or see and what they do.
- They have stimuli they can use to re-tell stories, make up stories, and re-enact stories.

Literacy-enriched play makes a wonderful contribution to the literacy learning of young children and should play a central role in this process.

Bilingualism and literacy

What is bilingualism?

Bilingualism is the ability to speak two languages. However, it isn't as simple as that when we are dealing with the diversity of young children's lives and experiences. Many families and societies regularly use two, three or more languages. This is multilingualism, but it is now acceptable to refer to the ability to use several spoken languages and several written systems as bilingualism. Bilingualism in this broad sense is the normal thing for millions of people worldwide.

In fact, if we look at the world as a whole, people who only speak one language are in the minority. Most people speak two or more languages. These languages are learned easily in the first three years of life, which seems to be a sensitive period for language learning. It helps the child if each language is associated with a person, a place or a situation.

When we start to think about bilingualism, it is important not to be sidetracked by ideas about 'perfect' bilinguals as the only ones who qualify for the title! None of us are perfect in any language as there is always more we could learn about the spoken and written forms of a language, even the languages we call our 'mother tongues' or 'home languages'. Not all languages will be used in the same way. Some may be oral only, some will only be used in written form. Some people in the family may be 'receptive' bilinguals, in other words, they can understand another language but they may not have productive ability in that language. Some language will only be used in certain contexts, for example, temple or synagogue, or with certain people.

Young bilinguals will have a range of constantly changing abilities in speaking their languages. They usually have particular languages for particular people and situations and are skilled at 'switching' languages as the need arises. Some children might speak English in nurseries, day care centres, pre-schools and schools; use Turkish with their parents and grandparents; but live in a small neighbourhood dominated by Italian speakers and written Italian advertising. This kind of diversity also applies to written languages. Some languages do not have a written form; some written languages are kept for sacred writings; some written systems use pictures and signs; some people can read a language they do not speak; and it is quite common to speak a language but not be able to write it.

Facts about language and young bilinguals

All human languages are complicated systems for communicating and thinking. All human languages have patterns and rules and all languages can meet the needs of their speakers.

Learning more than one language at home, or a subsequent language in early care and education settings, is broadly similar to learning a first language in a monolingual home. Babies start by sharing meaningful and enjoyable activities with their carers and tuning in to the sounds of the languages that accompany these experiences. Babies and toddlers begin to say single words and then produce meaningful combinations of two, three and more words as they make sense of the languages and activities they enjoy and understand.

This very complex process is possible because all babies are born with a general language ability, or language instinct (Pinker, 1994). Young bilinguals are only different because they have two or more linguistic and cultural ways of using this innate ability.

Young bilinguals learning other languages use a 'bridge-building' strategy that gets them from a language they know well to the new language. They will start to use actual words from the new language but keep to the grammatical rules of a familiar language.

This is just a temporary stage; linguists call it 'interlanguage' (Selinker, 1992). It seems to be an excellent way of quickly getting to grips with a new language.

There is no truth in the idea that using more than one language reduces a child's ability in each of these languages. The mind does not have a limited capacity for processing languages and bilingualism must never be thought of as an educational handicap. In today's global community, it can be a great advantage to be bilingual, and for some professions or positions, it is a requirement.

Bilingualism has many advantages for the individual, especially when acquiring literacy. Young bilinguals know that there are many different ways of labelling the world and communicating meanings. They can investigate and compare the sounds, meanings and written forms of their different languages. This potential for thinking about languages as systems launches them into approaching writing and reading as just another system to investigate and unpack.

Young bilinguals are very aware of the gestures, tunes and sounds of their different languages. They are also sensitive to the different personal relationships and social situations that call for one language rather than another. There is research suggesting that bilingual children are more flexible thinkers and better problem-solvers, because they know from a very early age that there are different ways of doing things.

A particular language links all of us to particular people, communities, beliefs and stories. This is what we mean by culture. The bilingual shares the culture of more than one human group and has the possibility of a very rich and varied life.

Supporting young bilinguals

The key to success in working and learning with young bilinguals is respecting and welcoming their languages and their ways of life. We can do this by celebrating their festivals and sharing their foods, songs, dances and stories. We can learn a few useful words and phrases in their languages. We can be sensitive to the kinds of pictures, books, furnishings and photos that will help them to feel at home in a setting. The children's families and communities are a wonderful source of language and cultural knowledge. They can be invited in to cook, dance or sing with all of the children (not just those speaking the same language); they can tell stories in their own languages, or teach the children to count and write in different ways. They may be willing to teach the children traditional rhymes and games, or paint and draw, or just talk.

Experiences with bilingual people, and with books reflecting many different ways of life can broaden our own knowledge and attitudes and those of the monolingual children. It is very valuable learning for monolingual children to experience different languages and ways of writing things down from what they are used to. This is an important part of their literacy learning. It also helps them develop empathy with and an understanding of others, which helps develop an environment that is supportive of all children.

The planned activities in good early years settings are particularly helpful to young bilinguals learning a new language because they focus on play and investigations, active hands-on learning and lots of talk about people, objects and actions. Just like carers at home, early years professionals can be great language models and tutors. We can provide lots of repetition when children are first learning English by using the same phrases to refer to the same activity until the children understand what is meant. Later, we can say similar things in several different ways: 'We have to clear up in ten minutes'; 'It will soon be time to put the bricks away'; 'Please start to tidy up now'; 'Let's pack up now'; 'Have you put away your toys?' This kind of repetition and variation also models common English phrases for the children so that they hear new language forms that they can experiment with and imitate. Good professionals are also unconsciously demonstrating the kinds of gestures and body language that give helpful clues about word meanings.

Talk must be at the heart of any early years programme and adults who work with children need to think about how their own talk can help all the children, because they are all language learners. We have to ask ourselves if we use enough helpful facial expressions, eye contact, gesture and body movement, singing and mime. Are our voices clear and our speech unhurried? We mustn't exaggerate and shout at the children as if they were excitable dogs, or talk so slowly that we sound like idiots ourselves. Young bilinguals need to hear the natural rhythms, tones and pitch of ordinary English in use so that they can tune in to the language. We can increase the amount and variety of the language the children hear by having plenty of story and poetry audio tapes available; using story props and puppets; inviting visitors to the setting to talk with the children; and organising walks and visits to places outside. All these activities call for new words and language forms. Just think what you might talk about at the zoo, the beach or by the river.

All this exciting input is great but we must never push young children to speak a new language until they are ready. Remember that when babies are learning a first language they spend many months just observing and listening. We have to give that kind of protected space, time and caring support to young bilinguals. Children who enter a new context where a new language is spoken often go through what is sometimes called the 'silent period'. This may last for several months and sometimes worries the child's carers. Usually, however, the children are learning a great deal during this period by listening and watching what is happening. They need to be encouraged, but not pushed, to use the new language. They will do so when they are ready. The important thing is to make sure they are interested and actively learning, not withdrawn. You can see this in their eye movements, their body language, their facial expressions. Children who are withdrawn and unhappy will need help, which can come from discussing the situation with families, providing some bilingual support, encouraging other children to involve the child in their play, and making sure they know they are welcomed and liked.

Supporting bilingual families

In English-speaking countries, many bilingual parents worry about what language they should speak at home, since they want to make sure they give their child the ability to speak English fluently. The important issue is their long-term goals for the child. If they want the child to grow up speaking English only, as may be the case for some political refugees, for example, then the whole family may be in the process of shifting from one language to another. If both parents speak different languages, they may want the family language to be their shared language, English.

However, many families hope that their child will grow up able to speak both (or more) languages. They want their children to be aware and proud of their heritage and to be able to communicate easily with family members who may not speak English. They may see personal enrichment or professional advantages for their children to grow up speaking two or more languages fluently. If this is the case, it is important for them to maintain the home language. English is such a powerful language in the UK and Australia that it is unlikely that their children will not learn it. It is often the other family languages that need support, and families should be encouraged to maintain these at home and in the community, if they want their child to grow up bilingually.

Some early childhood educators may find it difficult to communicate with families when there is not a shared language. There may be bilingual speakers who can help. Where there is not, photos of the children taken during the day in various activities, and examples of the child's artwork or class-made books can provide a shared context to develop an atmosphere of mutual support.

Literacy learning happens in all languages and a positive approach to diversity supports all children's literacies.

6.1 Emma is learning to write both Chinese and English

Special needs and literacy

Choosing the right words

There is considerable disagreement about what are the acceptable words to describe children (and adults) who may have a complex range of physical, emotional, cognitive and social problems. The term 'disabled children' is increasingly used by disabled adults themselves and the professionals who work with disabled children and their families. The phrase 'children with special needs' is still widely used, particularly in care and education, and we will retain that usage because it is so familiar. However, we must emphasise the fact that all children have special needs, desires and potential and these special needs can change and vary at different times in their lives and developmental stages. We would also acknowledge that the term 'disabled' is a useful reminder of the fact that organisations like nurseries, schools, workplaces and society at large can sometimes 'disable' children and adults, often unintentionally.

The need for practitioners to be totally positive and pro-active in supporting the literacy development of all young children, whatever problems and disabilities they appear to have, is central to our approach. Disability is just one part of the diversity of human life and should not be seen as an acceptable reason for depriving young children of their right to be literate.

In this book, we have included in our definition of literacy more than just paper-based reading and writing. We have included talking, listening, visual literacy and techno-literacy. The underlying element in all of these aspects of literacy is communication. For many children, conventional communication may pose some challenges. This may be because of physical or mental challenges, for example, cerebral palsy, vision or hearing impairment, Down's Syndrome, autism, learning disabilities, chronic health problems such as asthma, or other circumstances that require attention. It may be that children have special gifts or abilities that pose challenges for their social integration into a peer group.

The task of early childhood educators is complex and challenging, as well as deeply rewarding, and an important aspect of educational planning focuses on meeting the individual needs of children and families. All children need opportunities to interact with others, have access to texts, take part in meaningful and appropriate literacy experiences and have their literacy learning supported by knowledgeable early childhood educators. All children's literacy learning is most strongly supported when there are mutually reinforcing partnerships between staff in educational settings and children's families. For children with special needs, this partnership is often extended to include experts in various areas, visiting teachers, teachers' aides and so on.

Over the last few years, policies in many countries have shifted from providing for children with special needs in separate educational settings to 'mainstreaming' or 'inclusive education', in other words, including special needs children in mainstream educational settings, usually with additional support provided in terms of additional staff with special education training. All children will benefit from a print-rich, interactive environment and this is an important equal opportunities issue for care and education settings. So, let's think about some strategies for making literacy learning more inclusive and accessible to children with special literacy needs.

The importance of high expectations

Not too long ago, and, in some cases, even today, families and educators often had low expectations for children with special needs. The focus tended to be on the problem and how to cope with it, with physical considerations a main focus of attention. However, attitudes have begun to change from a deficit approach, in which the focus is on what the child cannot do, to a positive approach which focuses on what the child *can* do and on how to extend this.

Children tend to accept external evaluations. All children can and should progress in their understandings, skills and abilities, without the handicap of being in the company of educators who focus on their limitations rather than their abilities. It is extremely important for their early childhood educators to provide stories, songs, books, literacy-enriched play, and other literacy experiences for all children, and to do their best to ensure that all children develop a positive view of themselves as learners. Dorothy Butler has written an inspiring book (1979) about how her disabled grandchild learned to read with the assistance of skilled and caring adults who loved picture books and shared them with her from birth.

Lowered expectations of children with special needs may result in their being offered less rich literacy experiences, or repetitive, decontextualised skill and drill activities. A 'mastery' approach, which focuses on the sub-skills of literacy, can further disadvantage these children by reducing the print-rich, language-rich, play-rich environment that engages and excites children and motivates them to learn more.

Language development

Language development and phonological awareness are important predictors of successful school literacy. Children who are hearing or vision impaired will need additional support in the form of alternative ways of accessing literacy, for example, through Braille, hearing aids, signing, lip-reading, access to talking books and enlarged print. The explosion in technology over the past few years has offered many new ways to support children with special needs, for example, cochlear implants, voice recognition software, concept keyboards.

Children who are deaf and learn to use sign language seem to go through a similar pattern of learning to communicate as hearing children. For example, they use names instead of pronouns initially, even though the signs for the pronouns (like 'me' and 'you') seem easier. They sign 'telegraphically' like hearing children. They invent words and over-generalise.

Children with physical disabilities may need a modified environment, both inside and in the outside area, in which they can get around independently. This may mean ensuring that there is room for a wheelchair. In some cases, existing equipment may need to be adapted or new equipment introduced. Consultation with experts in special education is essential. It is of critical importance that children with physical disabilities can interact with other children, access writing materials, listen to tapes, enjoy interactive CD-ROMS, have a turn on the computer and explore books – all of the language-based activities that build strong language foundations.

Children with exceptionally well-developed language skills may be already reading and writing before they enter school. There are many disturbing anecdotal accounts of children who learn that this is not expected of them and who hide their abilities. They may become bored or disruptive and may be lonely, with few close peer relationships.

Early childhood settings in which individual differences are not only accepted but valued, and in which there is an atmosphere of communal exploration and discovery in which each individual can make a valuable contribution, support the literacy learning of all children.

Partnerships

Children with moderate to severe disabilities may have these disabilities diagnosed at birth, or, in some cases, when they begin to attend early childhood settings. Educators may notice things about individual children that have been taken for granted, such as inaccurate pronunciation of sounds, reluctance to talk, or persistent rubbing of the ears. Good relationships with families offer opportunities to share observations. It can be very useful for families to know where they can go for additional assistance to see if there is anything that needs to be addressed through special intervention, individualised programmes or so on.

If early childhood educators are aware of any programmes or home practices that have been recommended to parents by specialists, they can try to both support these and also look for ways to provide a balance. For example, families who have to spend hours each day on physical therapies for children may have little time for reading and singing to their child. Families who are keen for their child to be able to read and write as early as possible may see limited value in role-play, singing and story-telling. Trusting relationships, in which families and early childhood educators can share their concerns, while knowing that they all want to support the child and build strong literacy foundations, benefit all children. Partnerships are strengthened if contact is also established between specialists such as speech pathologists/ therapists or physiotherapists and the staff in early childhood settings.

Parents, early years practitioners and other professionals can work together to share their expertise and support and value the individual differences, special needs and disabilities of all children who come through the doors of early years settings.

Assessment of children's literacy

What do we mean by assessment?

Put simply, assessment tells us if what we have planned and done has been effective. We ask ourselves 'assessment questions' about how effective we have been every time we wash a floor or change a light bulb. In these examples the answers are fairly obvious – the floor looks cleaner and the light works again! But when it comes to asking what young children are learning, or if they are learning what we have planned for them, it is no longer simple or obvious. However, it is very interesting and often exciting. The most important thing to remember is that assessment in the realms of child development, literacy and education is not about exact measurements, it is about making sound judgements.

Some features of educational assessment

We will examine five features of effective educational assessment before looking at some useful ways of assessing young children's language and literacy development.

1   Assessment has to be rooted in everyday reality and it should be going on all the time. Effective assessment is about trying to understand the particular children we are working with in a particular setting. It is no use if it is a big performance put on to impress others on a few occasions. The everyday reality of assessment means that we must try to find ways of including the children's views about what they are learning and how they feel about it. Some settings give the children disposable cameras so that they can record the things that are best, worst or important for them. Other practitioners use children's drawings and discussions with the individual children about how it feels to be a child in this place. Some exciting work is now being done using child-led 'tours' of settings and the making of 'maps' about good, bad and uninteresting places in the early years environment (Clark and Moss, 2001). This might not seem to be about straightforward assessment, but these are important new ways of listening to children and finding out their views about what adults think is going on.

ssessment by adults must be based on careful observations of
children. Observations can be written down, recorded on video
and supported by photographs, transcripts of children's talk
and sketches of their models, constructions and movements.
The skills of being a good child-watcher can be learnt by plenty
of practice in nurseries, homes, playgrounds, parks, beaches,
trains, buses, markets and shops. In some of these public places
it may not be wise or convenient to use a camera or write down
your observations, but you can train yourself to listen and
watch closely. You need to be able to pick up on 'critical
moments' when a child or baby appears to make some kind of
'breakthrough' in understanding, as demonstrated by gesture
and expression, a new physical skill, vocalisations or verbal
comments. If you are observing a child you know well, you may
start to identify regular patterns of behaviour. These might
include such things as hiding toys and objects in bags and
boxes, or being fascinated by strings, ribbons, hanging light
cords and shoelaces. These are called 'schemas' and reveal a
child's favourite way of exploring the world and thinking about
it. You may also begin to realise that a child you observe
regularly has some very characteristic ways of responding to
experiences. These include such personal styles of learning as
persistence, curiosity and co-operation and are known to early
years specialists as 'dispositions'. They too have important
implications for assessment because they indicate how a child
will approach learning and schooling.

3 All our observations are useless if we don't use them.
Observation must be thought about, or reflected on, because we
have to ask ourselves the big question, 'What's going on here?'
If observations are to be turned into useful assessments we have
to interpret them. The most effective assessments of young
children's thinking and learning are probably reached as a
result of sharing our observations and interpretations with the
children's families and with other professional colleagues who
work with the children. The great advantage of these
collaborative kinds of assessment is that they give us much
fuller and more detailed pictures of children's abilities and
achievements, around the clock and in a great variety of
settings. Children's levels of understanding and sophisticated
thinking strategies are frequently missed by observers who only
know half of the story or only see half of the picture!

4 Assessment should be 'authentic' (Fleet and Lockwood, 2002). What this means is that we need to look for indications that children can operate effectively in everyday contexts involving literacy. This implies that children are observed in meaningful contexts that are grounded in everyday life. What children need will be different in different contexts. We talk to a politician, a relative and a good friend differently. We write a letter of complaint and a report differently. We may skim read a document to find one particular fact we are looking for, whereas we may read every word carefully in a letter outlining our duties in a new job. All of these are authentic examples of literacy, and we need to be able to do them well if we are to operate effectively in different contexts.

So what does this mean for young children? It means that we need to provide opportunities that let children show us what they know about literacy. Literacy-enriched play is a useful strategy. So are strategies that involve children in real-life literacy, for example, planning a parents' and grandparents' day at pre-school can involve invitations, displays, signs, shopping lists for morning tea and so on.

5 Assessment has to be put to good use. Effective assessment always points the way forward to better learning and teaching. After making some kind of assessment of a child or of an educational activity we have to ask ourselves, 'What comes next?' So the business of assessment is to take us forward in our thinking about the children and in our planning and practice. Effective assessment leads to new provision, new interventions and new experiences for the children.

Assessing language and literacy

If we are going to assess young children's communication, language and literacy development we must be able to:

- recognise it;
- record it;
- review it;
- share it.

Recognising it means that we must be open to what is happening when and where, and not be blinded by our own agendas or the pre-set goals of officials and politicians. We must understand and validate the wide range of language and literacy experiences that are part of society, including languages and dialects other than English, sign language, visual literacy, techno-literacy. Children may have a great deal of literacy knowledge that they are never given opportunities to display if early childhood educators do not ensure that links are made between children's individual interests and experiences, the literacy practices of their homes and communities and the literacy expectations of early childhood settings.

Young children have some uniquely personal ways of communicating, talking, marking and writing, sharing books and understanding languages. We need to tune in to children and recognise the 'critical moments' when they occur.

Dylan (2 years 9 months) is sitting on the bedroom floor waiting for his mum to finish dressing his baby brother. Mum hands him a book to look at and Dylan says, 'Shall I read it to you?' He turns to the first page of the book and reads, 'One day,' followed by very expressive 'blah-blah' vocalisations that reflect the tune of the story language. The noisy 'blah-blahs' are regularly interrupted by repetitions of 'one day' as he turns each page until he reaches the end of the book. He then says, 'It's the end' and shuts the book.

Dylan obviously knows a lot about reading a book: the traditional beginning; the sound of print being read; the turning of the pages; and the usual way of marking the end of a story. This is a critical piece of evidence that Dylan is on the way to becoming a reader.

Recording our observations, as the above example shows, is essential if we are to collect evidence of children's literacy development. We need to be as resourceful as possible in our recording, using written down or taped notes, stories and anecdotes, as well as photos, videos, diagrams and sketches. All these observations must be named and dated and notes on the context or setting provided. Many educators set up a system of individual 'portfolios' for children. These can contain selections by children, educators and families. The portfolios provide opportunities to review, reflect on, share and celebrate children's literacy learning over time.

Reviewing and reflecting on our observations means that we have to go deeper and not be content with noting that little Dylan was 'cute' when he read his book! We have to think about our observations, look for patterns, and discuss them with a colleague and the child's family, carer or key worker in a setting.

Sharing and celebrating them involves us in spreading the good news about our observations and coming up with innovations, changes, repeated experiences and whatever may be appropriate. It is important to do this in relation to individual children. It is also valuable to use what is sometimes referred to as 'documentation' of the learning that takes place as a group of children working with early childhood educators explores a group interest such as an extension to the pre-school building, or a bird's nest found in the outdoor play area, or the effects of a fire in a community. Artefacts, snippets of conversation, photographs, examples of children's written recording can be displayed in ways that enable the children themselves to visit and reflect on their learning, as well as to make children's learning more visible to the wider community.

The purpose of assessment in early childhood settings is not to compare children with each other. It is not testing. Rather, it is a

6.2 Family drawing by Dylan

6.3 Drawing by Clair

way of developing relationships with children and their families that give us insight into the children's learning and into how this can be fostered in a community of learners.

Official curriculum frameworks

In many countries, early childhood educators now work within the context of guidelines or frameworks or curriculum documents that are sanctioned by governments. These always reflect certain views of how children learn, what they should learn and how they should learn it. Often there is no author's name so it may appear as if everyone accepts the information without question. However, all of these documents are written by people with certain views on education, just as we have ourselves.

Here, we present some different approaches to official curriculum frameworks to underline the point that such documents change over time, and reflect certain views and social goals. Educators need to think about such documents in relation to their own beliefs and experiences and have the courage to speak out if they do not agree.

Foundation Stage, England

This is a curriculum framework that sets out to create a distinct phase of early education and care for children in England between the ages of 3 and 5+. It applies to all pre-school groups who receive government nursery funding, as well as state maintained early childhood centres, nursery schools and classes and the Reception Year of state primary schools. It was introduced in September 2000, and the official *Curriculum Guidance for the Foundation Stage* (QCA/DfEE, 2000) document outlines a set of principles for early education and six curriculum areas of learning. There is also guidance on such crucial matters as play, working in partnership with parents, working with children with special needs and with children with English as an additional language.

The principles
These have been strongly influenced by good early years practice from many countries and emphasise a developmentally appropriate curriculum for young children, well-trained and experienced practitioners and the inclusion of all children, no matter how diverse their needs. Among the principles listed are:

- Early education should build on what children already know and can do.
- No child should be excluded or disadvantaged.
- Parents and practitioners should work together.
- The learning environment should be well-planned, well-organised and stimulating.

- Effective education requires practitioners who understand that children develop rapidly during the early years – physically, intellectually, emotionally and socially.

There are some radical aspects to this official guidance, for example, it emphasises the crucial role of play in children's early learning and their need for adequate space and stimulating outdoor learning areas that are carefully planned for and well-resourced. The importance of using informal teaching methods is emphasised again and again because young children learn by active 'hands on' experiences shared with other children and with knowledgeable and sensitive adults.

Six areas of learning
These curriculum areas have attracted most attention and are often the only thing practitioners know about the Foundation Stage guidance. They are:

- personal, social and emotional development;
- communication, language and literacy;
- mathematical development;
- knowledge and understanding of the world;
- physical development;
- creative development.

There are six related early learning goals that describe in detail what children might be expected to achieve in each of these areas by the end of the Foundation Stage when they will be just 5 or nearly 6 years old, depending on their birth dates. The guidance also describes 'stepping stones' of progress towards the goals and these are actual examples of children's skills, attitudes, knowledge and understandings. A Profile Assessment Scheme is completed by Reception teachers for every child at the end of the Foundation Stage. This is also based on observations and assessments in all the six curriculum areas.

Communication, language and literacy
This now includes as goals: respect for communication in every area of the curriculum; planning for and valuing speaking and listening; emphasising enjoyment of narrative, stories, poetry and

music; experimentation and play with the sounds of languages and with words and texts; creating a print-rich environment; and practitioners who model the use of language as a tool for thinking and demonstrate the uses of reading and writing.

Selected documents influencing early literacy learning in Australia and New Zealand

In Australia, it is different State governments rather than the Commonwealth government that determine curriculum. Some, such as the *Queensland Preschool Curriculum Guidelines* published in 1998, are mandatory – in other words, teachers are obliged to implement them, whether or not they agree with their direction or philosophy. Others, such as the New South Wales curriculum framework, *The Practice of Relationships*, published in 2001 by NSW Department of Community Services, Office of Childcare, are non-mandatory, so early childhood educators can choose to implement them or not, or to implement some parts of them, but not all.

Many of the documents developed for prior to school settings do not link closely with the curriculum documents used in formal schooling. However, the South Australia Department of Education, Training and Employment (2001) has developed a framework for teaching, learning and assessing children from birth to Year 12, in a continuum organised through four Curriculum Bands. In Queensland, the foundation learning areas link to the core Key Learning Areas of compulsory education in Queensland, which include thinking and communicating.

As in the English Foundation Stage, a focus on Thinking and Communication is included in South Australia's Early Years Band Birth to 3, which has three areas: the psychological self, the physical self, and the thinking and communicating self. The Early Years 3–5 has seven areas: Self and social development; Arts and creativity; Communication and language; Design and technology; Diversity; Health and physical education; and Understanding our world. In this, the South Australian document is close in many respects to Foundation Stage principles. The emphasis on technology is an important inclusion when we think about how much our literacy practices have changed over the past few years, with mobile telephones, the internet, digital videos and so on.

In contrast to the documents that focus on learning areas, the New South Wales Framework focuses on social values and relationships as being of primary importance in early childhood education. In particular, it lists:

- openness;
- diversity;
- respect for others and for the physical world;
- service, commitment to others' well-being and to the good of the community;
- connection, relationship and collaboration;
- feelings, as well as thought and behaviour, as ways of understanding and communicating;
- resilience and perseverance;
- beauty;
- thoughtfulness and critical reflection;
- continuous pursuit of knowledge and understanding.

While the English Foundation Stage appears to be based on a developmentally appropriate model, documents from Australia and New Zealand reflect more of a social-constructivist approach. Queensland's Preschool Curriculum Guidelines (PCG) suggest that the social-constructivist approach is a means of bridging the gap between the different social and cultural experiences of children's homes and communities and 'school-based' learning.

The PCG affirm that children's literacy learning begins at birth, and that children's knowledge of literacy in the broad sense is developed and refined through real-life experience and play within their family and community. Teachers are required to create a curriculum that is culturally inclusive, individually appropriate and socially relevant. They are encouraged to provide time and opportunity for children to explore literacy symbols, rather than pushing children to write letters and numerals before they show an interest in doing so or are physically able.

In South Australia, also, children are viewed as constructing their own knowledge and understanding. In the SACSA framework, it is acknowledged that, while children share social and cultural aspects of life around them, each child is unique and their development and learning are not linear. Language and communication are seen as much more than words.

SACSA highlights children's symbolic play as a basis for abstract thinking, because it is through interaction with various forms of written, spoken, visual or performed texts that children learn how meanings are made. Educators are seen to have an important role in creating an environment that scaffolds children's learning, through introducing new vocabulary, language structures, communication tools and strategies, and through extending the children's confidence in verbal, non-verbal and visual communication.

New Zealand, unlike Australia, has a national curriculum document, *Te Whariki* (Early Childhood Curriculum), published in 1996 by the New Zealand Ministry of Education. Since 1998, early childhood service providers have been required to base their educational programme on, or be consistent with, the principles of Te Whariki.

These include Empowerment, Holistic Development, Family and Community, and Relationships. The strands are Well-being, Belonging, Contribution, Communication and Exploration. In *Te Whariki*, children are encouraged to learn with and alongside others through active exploration of the environment, developing working theories for making sense of the natural, social, physical and material worlds.

Play is valued as meaningful learning, and the importance of spontaneous play is recognised as it provides children with opportunities to learn strategies for active exploration, thinking and reasoning.

The curriculum recognises that children's direction and speed of learning and growing fluctuate, and can be influenced by environmental factors such as location and people. They learn to communicate in many ways, and for their language to grow and develop in meaningful contexts, *Te Whariki* asserts that they must have a need to know and a reason to communicate.

Social constructivism and a view of literacy as social practice are strong in *Te Whariki* because of its basis in the Maori language and lifestyle. Australia's indigenous population is much more scattered, with many languages and much social disruption, which has interrupted and weakened many aspects of traditional life. There is no set curriculum for indigenous pre-schoolers, but there is a Preschool Profile for literacy and numeracy, that is based on whether children are dependent on adult modelling to complete various tasks, whether they can complete tasks in a shared environment, or whether they can complete tasks independently.

When we look at these sample documents, we can see certain themes running through them all – the importance of play, active learning, adult engagement with children and connection with the community. There is also a strong focus in many of the documents on the central role of symbolic knowledge. There are differences in the extent to which the different sets of literacy practices of various communities are acknowledged, accepted and built upon. Generally, although it is widely accepted that, in theory, diversity is a good thing, most documents give little guidance on how early childhood educators can support children's diversity, particularly in terms of bilingualism. There are also differences in the extent to which children are given flexibility to reach different milestones at different times. Documents in which literacy is seen as a continuum and which link prior to school learning and school learning in ways that accommodate the different forms and rates in which children learn, offer support for their literacy learning.

6.4 Pre-schoolers relax with books at the end of the day

7

Some useful resources

We hope that you have enjoyed this brief guide to how babies and young children can be helped to develop early literacy in the pre-school years. We also hope that you feel as excited by young children's potential for literacy learning as we are and now want to know more. This chapter of useful resources is an attempt to start you off on the adventure of finding out more about young children, their families and their language and literacy development. We begin with a further reading list that will introduce you to some more detailed books about these topics. We include some professional journals from the UK and Australia that will keep you up to date with what is going on in the early literacy and early childhood world. We then recommend some videos and a resource pack, followed by a list of useful addresses of organisations in Australia and the UK concerned with literacy and early childhood. Our starter collection of picture books is just intended to get you thinking about the great wealth of literature easily available for young children. It is definitely *not* an official list of 'approved' books and we do hope that you will share your own favourite books and stories with the children you know best. Finally, we include two examples of leaflets about early literacy prepared for parents in the UK and Australia.

Further reading

Barratt-Pugh, C. and Rohl, M. (eds) (2000) *Literacy Learning in the Early Years*. Crows Nest: Allen and Unwin.

Beecher, B. and Arthur, A. (2001) *Play and Literacy in Children's Worlds*. Newtown: PETA.

Campbell, R. (1999) *Literacy from Home to School. Reading with Alice*. Stoke on Trent: Trentham Books.

Clark, A. and Moss, P. (2001) *Listening to Young Children: The Mosaic Approach.* London: National Children's Bureau/Joseph Rowntree Foundation.

Cousins, J. (1999) *Listening to Four Year Olds*. London: National Early Years Network.

David, T., Raban, B., Ure, C., Goouch, K., Jago, M., Barrière, I. and Lambirth, A. (2000) *Making Sense of Early Literacy: A Practitioner's Perspective*. Stoke on Trent: Trentham Books.

Drummond, M.J. (1993) *Assessing Children's Learning.* London: David Fulton.

Early Childhood Education Forum (1998) *Quality and Diversity in Early Learning*. London: ECEF/National Children's Bureau.

Kenner, C. (2000) *Home Pages: Literacy Links for Bilingual Children*. Stoke on Trent: Trentham Books.

Makin, L. and Jones Diaz, C. (eds) (2000) *Literacies in Early Childhood: Changing Views, Challenging Practice.* Sydney: MacLennan and Petty.

Marsh, J. and Hallet, E. (eds.) (1999) *Desirable Literacies. Approaches to Language and Literacy in the Early Years.* London: Paul Chapman Publishing.

Martin, E. (1999) *Baby Games*. Marrickville: CHOICE Books.

Mukherji, P. and O'Dea, T. (2000) *Understanding Children's Language and Literacy*. Cheltenham: Stanley Thornes.

National Literacy Trust (2002) *Getting a Head Start: A Good Ideas Guide for Promoting Reading to Young Families.* London: Department for Education and Skills.

Ouvry, M. (2000) *Exercising Muscles and Minds: Outdoor Play and the Early Years Curriculum*. London: National Early Years Network.

Pahl, K. (1999) *Transformations: Children's Meaning Making in a Nursery*. Stoke on Trent: Trentham Books.

Schickedanz, J. (1999). *Much More than the ABCs*. Washington: NAEYC.

Wade, B. and Moore, M. (2000) *Baby Power: 'Give Your Child Real Learning Power!'* Handforth: Egmont World Limited.

Whalley, M. and Pen Green Centre Team (2001) *Involving Parents in their Children's Learning.* London: Paul Chapman Publishing.

Whitehead, M.R. (2002) *Developing Language and Literacy with Young Children.* London: Paul Chapman Publishing.

Children's books referred to in the text

Dr Seuss (1957) *The Cat in the Hat.* New York: Random House.

Edens, C. (1998) *The Glorious Mother Goose.* New York: Atheneum Books for Young Readers.

Hill, E. (1980) *Where's Spot?* London: Heinemann.

Hill, E. (1998) *Spot Visits His Grandparents.* Harmondsworth: Penguin Books.

Hutchins, P. (1999) *It's MY birthday!* London: Random House.

Newcome, Z. (1999) *Toddlerobics Animal Fun.* London: Walker.

Ormerod, J. (1998) *Peek-a-Boo!* Los Angeles: Dutton Books.

Potter, B. (1902) *The Tale of Peter Rabbit.* London: Warne.

Waddell, M. and Firth, B. (1988) *Can't You Sleep, Little Bear?* London: Walker.

Professional journals

Australian Journal of Early Childhood
Australian Early Childhood Association, Inc.
PO Box 105
Watson
ACT 2602
Email: aecanat@atrax.net.au

Australian Journal of Language and Literacy
PO Box 3203
Norwood
South Australia 5067
Email: alea@netspace.net.au

*Early Childhood Practice: The Journal for Multi-Professional
Partnerships*
54 Mall Road
London W6 9DG
UK

Journal of Early Childhood Literacy
Sage Publications
6 Bonhill Street
London EC2A 4PU
UK
www.sagepub.co.uk

Nursery World (weekly publication, UK)
Admiral House
66–68 East Smithfield
London E1W 1BX
www.nursery-world.com

Books for Keeps: The Children's Book Magazine (six issues a year,
UK) ISSN 0143-909X
6 Brightfield Road
Lee
London SE12 8QF
Email: booksforkeeps@btinternet.com

Videos

Involving Parents in Their Children's Learning at the Pen Green
Centre (2001).
Contact:
Research, Development and Training Base
Pen Green Centre for Under 5s and Their Families
Pen Green Lane
Corby
Northants
NN17 1BJ

Sing and Sign. Help your baby to communicate before speech.
Sacha Felix (2001)
www.singandsign.com

Tuning in to Children. Birth to Five Years (1996). BBC Education/
National Children's Bureau. ISBN 1 86000 015 0

Resource pack

Birth to Three Matters. A framework to support children in their
earliest years (2002).
London: Sure Start/Department for Education and Skills.

Useful addresses

Bookstart
For project information contact Book Trust (see below)

Book Trust
Book House
45 East Hill
London SW18 2QZ
www.booktrust.org.uk

National Children's Bureau
8 Wakley Street
London EC1V 7QE
www.ncb.org.uk

National Literacy Trust
Swire House
59 Buckingham Gate
London SW1E 6AJ
www.literacytrust.org.uk

ORIM Project: Opportunities to learn. Recognition and valuing
early achievements. Interactions with adults in learning
situations.
Modelling by adults of literacy and numeracy behaviours.
Department of Educational Studies
University of Sheffield
388 Glossop Road
Sheffield S10 2JA

PEEP Project: Peers Early Education Partnership
PEEP Information Office
The PEEP Centre
Peers School
Sandy Lane West
Littlemore
Oxford OX4 6JZ

Support at Home for Early Language and Literacies (SHELLS)
The Children and Education Research Centre
University of Newcastle
Ourimbah
NSW 2258
Email: shells@newcastle.edu.au

Storysacks
Storysack Enterprises Limited
210 Church Cottages
Winterbourne Monkton
Swindon
Wilts SN4 9NW

A starter collection of picture books

Ahlberg, Janet and Allan (1978) *Each Peach Pear Plum*. London: Viking Kestrel.
Ahlberg, Janet and Allan (1988) *Starting School*. London: Viking Kestrel.
Bang, Molly (1983) *Ten, Nine, Eight*. Harmondsworth: Penguin.
Blake, Quentin (1995) *Quentin Blake's Nursery Rhyme Book*. London: Cape.
Breinburg, Petronella and Lloyd, Errol (1973) *My Brother Sean*. Harmondsworth: Penguin.
Browne, Eileen (1994) *Handa's Surprise*. London: Walker.
Burningham, John (1970) *Mr Gumpy's Outing*. London: Cape.
Burningham, John (2000) *Husherbye*. London: Cape.
Clement, R. (2002) *Olga the Brolga*. Pymble: Angus and Robertson.
Cooper, Helen (1993) *The Bear Under the Stairs*. London: Doubleday.
Cooper, Helen (1998) *Pumpkin Soup*. London: Doubleday.
Dale, Penny (1988) *Ten in the Bed*. London: Walker.

Deacon, Alexis (2002) *Slow Loris*. London: Hutchinson.

Gleeson, L. (1992) *Mum Goes to Work*. Gosford: Scholastic.

Grey, Mini (2002) *Egg Drop*. London: Cape.

Hayes, Sarah and Ormerod, Jan (1988) *Eat Up, Gemma*. London: Walker.

Heap, Sue (1998) *Cowboy Baby*. London: Walker.

Hughes, Shirley (1981) *Alfie Gets in First*. London: Bodley Head.

Hutchins, Pat (1968) *Rosie's Walk*. Harmondsworth: Penguin.

McKee, David (1980) *Not Now, Bernard*. London: Andersen.

Oliver, Narelle (2001) *Baby Bilby, Where do You Sleep?* South Melbourne: Lothian Books.

Ormerod, Jan (1985) *The Story of Chicken Licken*. London: Walker.

Rosen, Michael and Oxenbury, Helen (1989) *We're Going on a Bear Hunt*. London: Walker.

Sendak, Maurice (1967) *Where The Wild Things Are*. Harmondsworth: Penguin.

Simmons, Jane (1998) *Come On, Daisy!* London: Orchard.

Tolstoy, Aleksei and Sharkey, Niamh (1998) *The Gigantic Turnip*. Bath: Barefoot Books.

Waddell, Martin (1992) *Owl Babies*. London: Walker Books.

Whybrow, Ian and Reynolds, Adrian (1999) *Harry and the Bucketful of Dinosaurs*. London: David & Charles.

Wormell, Chris (1999) *Blue Rabbit and Friends*. London: Cape.

Communicating with families about early literacy

Here are two examples of leaflets, one from the UK and one from Australia, that were specially written by the authors to help parents and other family members understand more about their children's early literacy development. They give practical advice on what parents can do to encourage and support their children and they also warn of the dangers of pushing young children too soon into formal literacy exercises.

A Parent's Guide to Early Literacy (UK)

[This guide was first published in *Nursery World* 21 February 2002 and I am grateful to the Editor for permission to reprint it here. Marian Whitehead]

Some parents believe that putting a child on a reading scheme as soon as possible will mean that they will do better at school later on – but this is not the case. In fact, pushing a child into formal reading and writing exercises too young can damage the development of literacy. A far more effective way of equipping your child with good literacy skills is by having fun! Some ideas for fun are suggested here.

How does literacy start?
Literacy – reading and writing – develops from communication, which can be spoken or unspoken. When your baby looks into your eyes and gives you a big smile, you can't mistake what he is trying to tell you. Babies use gestures, facial expressions and crying to communicate, and this ability will grow the more you respond in turn. As children get older they also communicate by talking, listening, playing, drawing and making marks.

Literacy has to be real for young children, so they need to see their carers writing shopping lists or emails and reading newspapers, letters, books and notices. And they need to get involved too.

Remember: The foundations of literacy are communication and talk, enjoying books and understanding that marks (such as letters and numbers), pictures and print carry messages.

Communication, language and literacy is one of the six areas of learning in the Foundation Stage for 3 to 5-year-olds in nurseries in England. Nursery staff will do similar activities to these.

What can I do at home?
- Introduce your child to picture books as a young baby. The secret is to be close and comfortable, turn the pages and talk about the pictures. Use the same books over and over again. Encourage your child to look closely at the pictures and touch the pages. Let them take books to bed and on car and bus rides, and join the local public library, especially if you cannot afford books. The national literacy trust (**www.literacytrust.org.uk**) has details of schemes that give free books to pre-schoolers.
- Spend time talking to your child – at mealtimes, bath times, when you are out and about. Make TV and video viewing a shared activity and talk about what you are watching.
- Sing nursery rhymes and advertising jingles. Play with words

and recite bits of poetry. This play with language will be the greatest contribution you can make to your child's understanding of the sounds of letters and words.

- Show your child the print on letters and food packaging and look at street names, posters, road and shop signs.
- Include your child in any writing you do – let them add scribbles to shopping lists and letters.
- Collect scrap paper for painting and drawing, as well as crayons and paints. Watch children make marks – on pastry and playdough, on outside surfaces with water and brushes, on wet sand in play areas or on beaches. Talk about these marks and treat them as serious communications.
- Put your child's name on paintings, cupboards and storage boxes.

Remember: Parents can be the best teachers of early literacy if they make it fun and get across a sense of real communication.

What about learning the alphabet, the sounds of letters (phonics), flash cards, reading schemes and tracing letters?
- Beautiful alphabet books can stimulate your child's fascination with the initial sounds and letters of familiar objects. Always talk about letters by name and by the 'sounds' they usually make.
- Flash cards are unhelpful – the best way for children to learn to recognise words is in meaningful contexts. For example, they will quickly recognise the name of their favourite breakfast cereal on the box.
- Avoid reading schemes – use picture and story books that stimulate children's imagination and foster a love of books.
- If children have ample opportunities to scribble, draw and paint, they don't need to trace letters. In fact, if they are pushed into copying writing too soon, it is likely to put them off.

Remember: Pushing a child into formal reading and writing exercises can damage the development of literacy.

Early Literacy – How Do We Provide the Best Start for Children?

[This guide was first published by the Centre for Community Child Health, Royal Children's Hospital, Melbourne, Australia, in September 1999 and I am grateful to the Centre for permission to reprint it here. Laurie Makin]

Literacy begins well before children start school. Children become literate as they take part in everyday experiences at home and in the community. Research shows that the first five years of life are particularly important for literacy development. Parents and early childhood staff can work together to promote literacy.

What does 'literacy' include?

In the past, literacy used to mean just reading and writing. Now, when people speak of literacy, they often include listening, talking, reading, writing, viewing and critical thinking.

Viewing has become important because of the widespread use of TV, videos and computers. Critical thinking has become essential, to access information and as a way of learning to cope with the sheer volume of information from TV, videos and computers. For example, very young children have to learn that toys advertised on TV may not look or act the same in real life.

How does your child's early childhood setting promote early literacy?

- Staff talk and read to your child every day. They tell stories and encourage the children to tell stories too. They have books and writing materials available for children to explore. They encourage play on real or imaginary computers. Literacy is part of many activities such as dramatic play (for example, acting out stories), construction (for example, road signs), and interest centres (for example, a shop or a hospital).
- Staff talk to the children about what they themselves are doing as they read a chart, write a list, use the computer and so on.
- Many activities do not involve literacy directly but they help develop knowledge and skills needed for literacy. Children learn to express their ideas in different forms, for example, drawing, painting and modelling with clay. They become aware of sounds through songs, rhymes and finger plays.
- Staff give you information about your child's language and literacy development. They ask you what you have noticed about your child's literacy experiences at home and in the community.

Is there any benefit in teaching children letters and writing before they start school?

Most children become interested in letters and writing somewhere between the ages of 4 and 7. There does not seem to be any benefit in pushing children to learn about letters before they are ready. They may feel inadequate and learn to avoid literacy activities if these are stressful experiences. Children need opportunities to explore written language and talk about it with adults. If as part of this exploration, children show interest in learning letter names – perhaps letters in their own name – or in writing, respond to these interests, but do not push!

What can I do at home to support my child's literacy?
Talk to your child about what you are doing as you read, write or view. Use literacy-related words. For example, you might say, 'Let's see, what do we need to buy today? I'd better write a shopping list. Where's the pencil?' or, 'I've forgotten what time that program on the Olympics comes on. Let's read the TV guide and see', or 'I think I'll email Dorothy. Let's turn on the computer.'

Read to your child. Introduce children to a wide range of books – storybooks, information books, fairy tales, counting books, alphabet books, songbooks. Read print around your neighbourhood. Take your child to the local library. Find out if they have story time. Borrow books regularly. You may also be able to borrow audio tapes, audio books and videos.

It isn't necessary to read at the same time every day or to read the same type of material every day, but it is good to give your child reading experiences at least daily and preferably much more often. Experiences can include books, magazines, labels on food packages, shop signs and numbers.

When you are reading, make the experience an interactive one. Relate what you read to what children know or do in their everyday lives. Talk about the pictures or the writing. Discuss what might happen next or how the characters feel or what else they could have done in a particular situation.

Use songs, rhymes and finger plays with your child. Give your child opportunities to scribble write. Children love to make their own shopping lists or write letters to grandparents, sign birthday cards and so on. You will be able to see, in your child's early scribble writing, what they have learned. Do they scribble in lines? Do they tell you what the scribble says?

Keep open the lines of communication with the staff in your child's early childhood setting. Ask what they are doing. Tell them what you are doing at home. Let children know that they will learn to read and write over time and that it is a very gradual process.

What about TV, videos and computers?
Know what your child watches and discuss what s/he sees. Help your child develop critical thinking by discussing reality/fantasy, different cultural practices and gender roles. This is important, even for very young children.

Encourage programmes/videos/computer games that are appropriate for your child's age and interests. Use TV, videos and computers as part of the whole range of literacy experiences that your child encounters. Try to balance time spent with these experiences.

What if we speak a language other then English?
If you want your child to keep your home language, use it as much as possible – at home and in the community. Look for support outside your home – friends, community groups, videos, movies.

Staff can help your child feel comfortable about speaking two (or more) languages. You may be able to help them include your home language and culture as part of your child's everyday experiences in the early childhood setting. Staff may use familiar words, greetings or songs which will greatly enhance bilingual skills, especially in settings where there are many languages represented.

Key points to remember

- Your child develops literacy through talking and sharing information with people who are important in their life.
- The process of developing literacy starts at birth and is a gradual one.
- In the pre-school years, children learn that print is all around them. It is meaningful, functional and enjoyable.
- Staff and parents are partners in the process of children's literacy development.

References

Barratt-Pugh, C. (2002) 'Children as writers', in L. Makin and C. Jones Diaz (eds) *Literacies in Early Childhood: Changing views, challenging practice*. Eastgardens: MacLennan and Petty. pp. 93–116.

Berndt, T. (1997) *Child Development*. 2nd edn. Dubuque: Brown and Benchmark.

Butler, D. (1979) *Cushla and Her Books*. Sevenoaks: Hodder & Stoughton.

Clark, A. and Moss, P. (2001) *Listening to Young Children: The Mosaic Approach*. London: National Children's Bureau.

Department for Education and Skills (DfES) Sure Start Unit (2002). *Birth to Three Matters: A Framework to Support Children in their Earliest Years*. London: DfES.

Fleet, A. and Lockwood, V. (2002) Authentic literacy assessment. In L. Makin and C. Jones Diaz (eds) *Literacies in Early Childhood: Changing Views, Challenging Practice*. Eastgardens: MacLennan and Petty, pp. 135–153.

Fox, M. (2001) *Reading Magic*. Sydney: Pan Macmillan.

Goldschmied, E. and Jackson, S. (1994) *People Under Three: Young Children in Day Care*. London: Routledge.

Gopnik, A., Meltzoff, A. and Kuhl, P. (1999) *How Babies Think: The Science of Childhood*. London: Weidenfeld and Nicolson.

Griffiths, N. (1997) *Storysacks: A Starter Information Pack*. Swindon: Storysack National Support Project.

Hill, S., Comber, B., Louden, W., Rivalland, J. and Reid, J. (1998) *100 Children go to School: Connections and Disconnections in Literacy Development in the Year Prior to School and the First Year of School*. Vol. 1. Canberra: DEETYA.

Makin, L. and Jones Diaz, C. (eds) (2002) *Literacies in Early Childhood: Changing Views, Challenging Practice.* Eastgardens: MacLennan and Petty.

Makin, L. and Whiteman, P. (2002) 'Literacy, music and the visual arts', in L. Makin and C. Jones Diaz (eds) *Literacies in Early Childhood: Changing views, challenging practice.* Eastgardens: MacLennan and Petty, pp. 289–304.

Marsh, J. (1999) 'Teletubby tales. Popular culture and media education', in J. Marsh and E. Hallett (eds) *Desirable Literacies: Approaches to Language and Literacy in the Early Years.* London: Paul Chapman Publishing.

New South Wales Office of Child Care (2001) *A Framework for Constructing Meaning. Rationale for the Practice of Relationships: Essential Provisions for Children's Services.* Sydney, NSW: NSW Department of Community Services.

New Zealand Ministry of Education (1996) *Te Whariki: Early Childhood Curriculum.* Wellington: Learning Media.

Nutbrown, C. (1999) *Threads of Thinking: Young Children Learning and the Role of Early Education.* 2nd edn. London: Paul Chapman Publishing.

Pinker, S. (1994) *The Language Instinct. The New Science of Language and Mind.* Harmondsworth: Penguin.

Qualifications and Curriculum Authority (QCA) and DfEE (2000) *Curriculum Guidance for the Foundation Stage.* London: QCA.

Queensland School Curriculum Council (1998) *Preschool Curriculum Guidelines.* Brisbane: Queensland Office of the Queensland School Curriculum Council.

Selinker, L. (1992) *Rediscovering Interlanguage.* London: Longman.

South Australia Department of Education, Training and Employment (2001) *Early Years Band: Early Years Band Age 3–Age 5. South Australian Curriculum Standards and Accountability (SACSA).* Adelaide: South Australia Department of Education, Training and Employment.

Sulzby, E. (1985/1994) 'Children's emergent reading of favorite storybooks: A developmental study', *Reading Research Quarterly,* 20: 458–481. Republished with update in, R.B. Ruddell, M.R. Ruddell and H. Singer (eds) *Theoretical Models and Processes of Reading.* 4th edn. Newark: International Reading Association. pp. 244–280.

Teale, W.H. and Sulzby, E. (eds) (1986) 'Emergent literacy: Writing and reading.' Volume in series, M. Farr (ed.) *Advances in Writing Research.* Norwood, NJ: Ablex.

Whalley, M. and Pen Green Centre Team (2001) *Involving Parents in their Children's Learning.* London: Paul Chapman Publishing.

Whitehead, M. (2002) 'Dylan's routes to literacy: the first three years with picture books'. *Journal of Early Childhood Literacy,* 2 (3): 269–289.

Index

assessment, 2, 66, 77, 95–9
  authentic, 97
  definition, 95
  features, 95–7
  and literacy, 97–100
  observations, 96, 98–9, 102

bilingualism, 2, 65, 81, 106
  definition, 85–6
  interlanguage, 86–7
  learning English, 88–90
  and literacy, 85–90
  partnerships with families, 4,
    24–5, 89–90, 118
Birth to Three Matters, 16–17, 111
brain studies, 16, 28, 29, 49
book(s),
  area, 63
  and babies, 8, 15, 21–8, 81, 114
  book handling skills, 41, 73–4
  collections, 57, 107, 112–13
  and language development, 3, 6,
    32–8
  language of, 22, 73, 74
  making, 35, 67, 72, 83
  non-fiction, 57, 59, 117
  outdoor use, 62, 83
  picture, 15, 21–2, 31, 41, 48, 56, 59,
    114, 115, 120
  reading schemes/primers, 15,
    56, 113, 115

sharing, 21–8, 34, 38, 41, 56, 92,
    107, 114, 117
  sense of story, 73, 74
Bookstart, 22, 111

communication, 10, 15, 91, 114–15
  between infants and carers,
    5–6, 11–12, 16, 17–21, 114,
    117
  non-verbal, 5, 7, 19, 88
  signing, 4–5, 18, 19, 28, 50,
    93, 98, 110
  and talk, 20–1, 32–8, 50–1, 82,
    88, 114, 116, 117
curriculum, 2, 47, 64, 66
  official frameworks in
    Australia and New Zealand,
    47, 103–6
  official frameworks in the UK,
    47, 100–2, 103
  'push-down', 75, 79

dispositions, 47, 51, 64, 65, 66, 76,
    77, 79, 96

Foundation Stage, England,
    101–3, 104, 114

invented spelling, 72

key practitioners, 23, 24

language,
   and communities, 32, 65, 73, 87–8
   development, 13, 20–1, 30, 32–8,
      45–6, 86–7, 93–4, 115
   in homes, 32, 89–90, 118
   play, 27, 33, 41, 81–2, 88, 114, 116,
      117
literacy,
   critical, 7, 116
   definition, 7–9, 91, 114, 116
   emergent, 9, 10, 69–75
   –enriched play, 67–9, 76, 81–5,
      97
   in families and communities, 3–6,
      27, 42–3, 106, 113–18
   individual differences in, 3–5,
      69–75
   learning, 5–9, 47–59, 69–79, 84–5
   and life opportunities, 9, 29,
      76–7, 87, 91
   out-of-doors, 62, 83
   in preschools and nurseries,
      45–63, 114, 116
   and problem solving, 68–9
   and reading 'readiness', 56–7
   snapshot, 13–14, 43–4, 59–60, 79–80
   as social practice, 9, 10, 12, 32,
      33, 42, 51, 53, 76, 82–3, 97, 105,
      114
   techno–, 7, 42, 91, 98
   visual, 7, 91, 98, 116

New South Wales' curriculum framework, 103

observation, 69, 99

partnerships,
   families, 39, 75–9, 87–8, 94
   early years' teachers, 79
   transition to school, 76–7
   specialists, 4–5, 94
phonological awareness, 33
play,
   adult role, 27, 67, 69, 84
   imagination, 37
   learning, 82, 105
   literacy, 37, 74, 82–5
   talk, 27

   role play, 37
   socio-dramatic, 67, 69, 82–4
popular culture, 68

Queensland Preschool Curriculum
   Guidelines, 103, 104

reading, 21–3, 35
   decoding, 73
   emergent, 72–3
   intonation, 73, 74
   book language, 73
record keeping, 13, 27, 43, 79, 97–9
rhyme, poetry and song, 27, 37–38,
   117

schemas, 96
South Australia's curriculum
   framework, 103, 104
special needs, 91–4
   language development, 93
   expectations, 92
   partnerships, 92, 94
story,
   props, 74
   reading, 23, 34
   telling, 35, 74
   traditional, 96

talking and listening,
   babies, 8, 11–12, 17–21, 42
   toddlers, 32–5, 38, 39
   young children, 12–13, 88–9, 114,
   117
technology,
   television and video, 42, 116–7
   computers, 3, 72
   audio tapes, videos and DVDs, 42,
      110
Te Whariki, New Zealand, 105
text types, 33

writing and print, 10, 71–2
   activities, 12, 35, 43, 83, 114, 117
   socio-dramatic play, 37, 67, 72, 75,
      82–4
   emergent, 69–72
   materials, 25
   scribbling, 9, 40, 43, 69